Negotiation
Shielded against manipulation

The fallacy of win-win

HARCORE

Author: Mauricio Furtado

Carlos Mauricio Furtado

Negotiation: Shielded against manipulation
The fallacy of win-win

1st Edition

The 1st edition brings emotional and rational approaches with a focus on expanding the ability to define one's own negotiations and, most importantly, not being manipulated by others.

ISBN: 9798863744070

Independent Publication

Author's Note

Negotiating is about positioning oneself in relationships; however, in a business environment, understanding the rational direction of a negotiation anticipates strategies and plans.

This book was written for any professional looking to enhance their emotional and analytical capacity in commercial negotiations.

Mauricio Furtado

Indice

[Introduction] The fallacy of 'win-win"

[Part 1] Awareness of Emotion

[Chapter 1] Nonverbal Communication

[Chapter 2] Irrationality

[Chapter 3] Influence and Manipulation

[Parte 2] The Power of Reason

[Chapter 4] Logic and Critical Thinking

[Chapter 5] Statistics and Probability

[Chapter 6] Game Theory

[Part 3] The Art of Agreement

[Chapter 7] Procrastination and Cognition

[Chapter 8] Focus and Consequence

[Introduction] The fallacy of 'win-win"

"The fallacy of false analogy is often used to make simplistic arguments appear more persuasive than they really are."

In 1983, Freddy Heineken, the owner of Heineken brewery, was kidnapped in the city of Amsterdam along with his driver Ab Doderer, by four kidnappers, and was held captive for 11 days. The kidnappers demanded a ransom of $35 million, equivalent to $14 million, and after a series of negotiations with the police, the ransom was paid, and Heineken and Doderer were released. The kidnappers carefully prepared the hideout for the victims and negotiated directly with the police and family members. However, the lack of police preparedness in dealing with the abduction and the ineffective communication between the negotiation team and the police resulted in a backup plan, in which the ransom was paid without police supervision and authorization. This prevented the capture of the kidnappers. Hostage negotiations set a hostile environment with disproportionate losses on both sides, making business negotiations seem trivial in comparison. While hostage negotiations deal with life and death, business negotiations deal with more or less profit.

Negotiating with opponents who seemingly have nothing to lose complicates the understanding of the 'win-win' concept, turning it into a fallacy, an illusion in the eyes of those who achieved greater success in the negotiation. In Freddy Heineken's case, it could be said that there was a 'win-win' outcome, as the kidnappers obtained the $14 million they intended, and Mr. Heineken emerged unharmed. However, for external observers, the kidnappers should have been arrested, or perhaps they could have demanded a higher amount, given the billionaire fortune of the Heineken family. The fact is that the 'win-

win' negotiation involves expectations, emotions, values, and prejudices in a complex environment, often surrounded by irrationality, attachments, and historical context. In this scenario, for there to be a winner, there must be a loser.

When loss results from fraud or bad faith, it's emotionally difficult to comprehend the 'win-lose' concept. This occurs, for instance, when a company offers a salary below the market average to an unemployed candidate, or when a buyer takes advantage of the urgency and financial difficulty of the seller to acquire a property below market value. Similarly, a distributor that significantly raises prices upon noticing a scarcity of a particular raw material in the market also fits into this scenario. Traditional economics treats the supply-demand relationship as a science that defines an equilibrium price when the supply and demand curves become imbalanced. Human and corporate greed will always seek opportunities to tip agreements toward 'win-lose' situations, labeling them as 'win-win'.

In the absence of reason, it's possible to consider an unemployed individual a winner when compared to having no income at all. Likewise, it's possible to acknowledge the goodwill of a real estate buyer who acquires a property below market value and enables the seller to settle debts. Moreover, it's possible to perceive a distributor as a business partner who, by selling raw materials at disproportionate prices, helps the customer meet their clients' demands. The 'win-win' concept is merely a point of view when rationality isn't attributed to agreements."

Authors and negotiators from the FBI, specialized in hostage negotiations, recognize a "win-win" situation when both parties feel that their needs and interests have been met. A successful hostage negotiation considers effective communication and the building of trust as essential attributes for problem resolution. To achieve this, they understand the motivation and flexibility of the kidnappers. On the other hand, authors of business negotiations perceive mutual cooperation, strategic relationships, and financial outcomes as the foundation of agreements.

Negotiations in commercial and critical environments deal with emotions and the rationalization of positions. There's an understanding of the context and the ability to adapt to unexpected circumstances. The book considers a commercial negotiation and presents rational models for defining context, positions, emotions, and the game that leads to a resolution. The concept of "win-win" is presented strongly, where prepared parties have a greater chance of understanding an agreement compared to parties driven by emotions, hierarchy, and external manipulation.

The book approaches negotiation through emotional aspects, exploring body language, situational hierarchy, human irrationality, and cognitive manipulation. It also employs a rational approach, evaluating pragmatic conditions of cooperation, positioning, and planning. Ultimately, the negotiation concludes by defining agreements and assessing whether the outcome was favorable for both parties or only for one of them.

[Part 1] Awareness of Emotion

"Until you become conscious, the unconscious will direct your life, and you will call it fate."

Carl Jung

In 2010, Adam Neumann brought the vision of flexible office spaces, a viable alternative for entrepreneurs, startups, and freelancers. The idea was well executed by Neumann, who strategically positioned WeWork in major metropolises, attracting the interest of a large number of clients, which boosted the coworking market. WeWork's growth was exponential, reaching a global scale with locations in New York, London, São Paulo, Tokyo, and Mexico City. However, the apparent success of WeWork contrasted with Neumann's emotional and extravagant management style. Emotion, just like rationality, is an important human characteristic, and a balance is necessary to ensure awareness and consequences of actions, especially in business. Neumann created an emotional environment where exponential growth was sustained without adequate financial backing, as the Vision Fund financed the operation; thus, unrestricted cash flow masked an unprofitable operation.

In 2019, WeWork was preparing for an initial public offering (IPO), and financial and accounting information was required, revealing Neumann's emotional management and lack of accounting skills, raising concerns among investors. The IPO was canceled due to concerns about the company's financial health, and Neumann was removed from the CEO position. The board of directors worked to regain market confidence in WeWork. The company's market value plummeted, and even though Neumann was the visionary behind WeWork's success, in a financial market environment where consistency, transparency in financial statements, and stability are more valued than bold management and entrepreneurial vision, emotion played a significant role. Emotion played a significant role in the creation and growth of WeWork but also generated negative perceptions about the company's governance.

Numerous negotiations filled Neumann's agenda, from the well-known practice of persuading real estate agencies and property owners to provide properties in exchange for profit sharing to negotiations with investors to keep the company running based on free cash flow for an extended period, as well as emotional pressures due to accounting differences, expense management, and revenue. Attention to numbers exposed WeWork to various financial vulnerabilities, even though emotionally, the public saw it as an innovative company with a disruptive business model. Emotion needs to align with reason to ensure strategic balance and stability.

[Chapter 1] Nonverbal Communication

"Our actions are the best interpretations of our thoughts."

(John Locke)

In 2002, Laci Peterson disappeared, and her husband Scott, when giving a statement to the police, displayed behavior inconsistent with the situation. His body language was disinterested, his tone and facial expression were inappropriate, and he referred to Laci in the third person. This initially turned him from an informant into the primary suspect. Body language wasn't sufficient evidence to incriminate Scott before the police. However, it was crucial in diverting attention and seeking compelling evidence that would prove his awareness and involvement in the crime, leading to his trial and subsequent life imprisonment.

The human brain is a stimulus receptor, converting stimuli into hormones for the purpose of human survival, a result of millions of years of natural genetic selection in homo sapiens. Fear stimulates the muscles and vision, releasing hormones like cortisol and adrenaline in abnormal amounts, priming the body for 'fight or flight.' Cortisol regulates metabolism, increasing blood sugar levels, while also suppressing the immune system, reducing inflammation, and facilitating artery dilation. Adrenaline, on the other hand, increases heart rate, readies the muscles, activates vision, and inhibits the digestive process to conserve energy. Bronchi dilate to allow greater oxygenation and energy production. The combination of cortisol and adrenaline is a subconscious survival process that can harm the immune and digestive systems and even cognitive function.

A human cannot suppress the hormonal production caused by external stimuli. These stimuli are electrical signals sent to the hypothalamus, which triggers an alert response in the body. The human body is a survival machine; thus, external stimuli like fear, stress, and anxiety are recognized by the amygdala and the prefrontal cortex, understanding and reacting to both real and imaginary threats. Each individual has their own way of absorbing these stimuli, influenced by experiences, values, and beliefs. In negotiations, social conventions suggest that individuals shouldn't show fear of a failed agreement. However, the body doesn't follow these conventions and somehow reveals the fear. Well-trained negotiators establish better self-control, strength, and intelligence through the constant connection between the conscious and subconscious minds.

Body language emphasizes nonverbal

communication, being a technique that identifies unconscious perceptions of the emotions of the other party. Negotiations with a 'win-lose' bias more easily reveal personal emotions, making fear and pleasure more readily noticeable. It's important to understand that the counterpart's body language isn't solely related to the negotiation context but also to the personality on the other side of the table. Narcissists seek attention and admiration; therefore, understanding who they want to impress helps anticipate their next moves. On the other hand, individuals with borderline personality disorder are unstable and impulsive, so closures need to be more carefully planned. There are also sociopaths, who have an antisocial personality and tend to show minimal emotion.

Body language is one of the tools in negotiation and can be displayed in various forms, such as eye contact, body posture, gestures, facial expressions, and voice tone. Each detail is important, as it will serve as the foundation for more assertive approaches. Eye contact establishes trust, and creating an atmosphere of honesty is critical in negotiations. Thus, it's important to understand when and how the counterpart is being untruthful. Through body posture, collaboration is defined, and it's relevant to establish ways in which the other party feels welcomed and intends to cooperate. Facial expressions determine the emotional response of the other party in milliseconds, and gestures of approval and disapproval can be perceived. Voice tone conveys confidence; therefore, changes in tone when discussing arguments and agreements are associated with nonverbal communication."

In April 2010, the live televised negotiation between Ukrainian government officials regarding cooperation with Russia in the leasing of the Sevastopol naval base in Crimea for 25 years was a spectacle. The parliamentarians exchanged punches and shoves, creating widespread chaos and clearly demonstrating the emotional conflict over defining terms. For the opposition, the agreement was seen as an affront to the country's sovereignty and foreign policy. However, the political strength of the pro-Russian party defined the 'win-lose' scenario, and Ukraine signed an agreement until 2042, benefiting from favorable natural gas prices. Before resorting to physical altercations, body language extends beyond micro-perceptions. Anger, an emotion stemming from frustration, reveals the weakness of the opposition in making decisions about the nation's interests.

Human behavior was studied by mathematician and psychologist Clark Hull, who provided insightful associations about human motivation. In 1943, he published the book 'Principles of Behavior,' where he stated that motivation is regulated by a complex set of factors. Hull's experiments were mathematically grounded, allowing for numerical associations in four elements. The first element was the degree of deprivation, which was central to the study and classified on a scale of 0 to 100. Hunger defined the degree of deprivation, and for Hull, the discomfort of intense hunger motivated individuals to do anything. The second element is the strength of the drive unit, referring to the effort exerted by the individual to alleviate deprivation. According to Hull, an individual exhibits a higher drive unit strength when correlated with deprivation. Therefore, significant efforts are only made when deprivation is proportional. The third element is the probability of success, defining how an individual relates effort to success. This element is linked to past experience, competence, and learning. Understanding what needs to be done to alleviate a degree of deprivation allows for the association of success level, strengthening motivation. The last element is the intensity of behavior and magnitude of reward, two interconnected concepts that relate to effort exerted and reward attributed. Gratification serves as a pleasure element in this context. Reward is a relevant factor in human motivation.

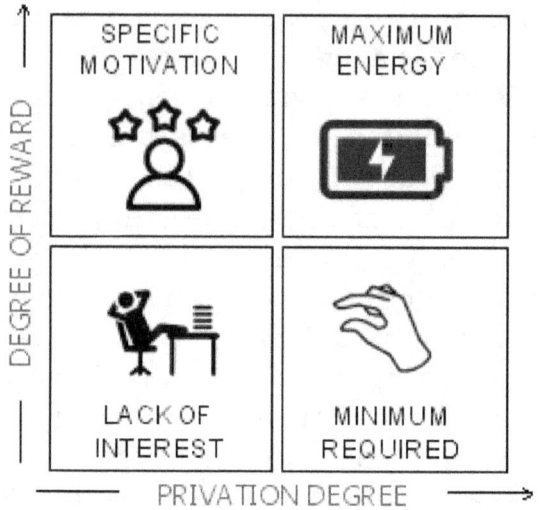

In business negotiations, Hull's findings can be associated with complexities that challenge the concept of 'win-win.' Motivation is individual, as there is no corporate entity. Thus, understanding how motivation operates in the counterpart defines relevant negotiation components. Deprivation can manifest as missed promotion opportunities or even job loss. In this concept, it's essential to grasp the counterpart's plea and associate it with possible deprivations."

In a negotiation, it's important to understand the motivations of both sides, anticipating emotional reactions when one of the parties holds greater commercial power. Motivation takes into account deprivations and rewards, and in a company composed of emotional individuals, understanding how the company reacts in unfavorable circumstances is crucial in setting the tone of the negotiation. Deprivation involves the company's inability to meet the demands of counterparts and controversial reactions driven by emotional aspects. A supplier may halt deliveries if the customer doesn't pay the requested increase, just as the customer may delay payments to suppliers to manage cash shortages. Unilateral actions that don't allow room for negotiation can generate emotional conflicts between the parties, resulting in unfavorable commercial and legal conditions for both.

American psychologist Abraham Maslow proposed a hierarchy of needs in 1954 that aligns well with deprivations and can be associated with challenging commercial negotiations. Maslow categorized motivation and deprivation into hierarchical levels of needs, starting with physiological needs, followed by safety, belongingness, esteem, and self-actualization. In difficult negotiations, emotional conditions complicate agreements, and negotiators representing a company must understand the motivations that limit decisions and build trust so that a "win-win" agreement can be achieved. Associating emotion and deprivation within a corporate context is not trivial, as many factors come into play. However, assessing reactions allows for shaping appropriate paths that facilitate an agreement.

Maslow views the first layer, physiological needs, as a survival layer, and companies in this layer are motivated by basic issues such as cash flows. In new businesses, these companies strive to offer the best conditions, but in ongoing agreements, they may try to modify pre-established deals. Deprivation of cash flow generates emotional situations that can define a state of "fight or flight." Negotiators and business leaders in this layer exhibit aggressive body language, as quick decisions benefiting cash flow are necessary.

The second need in Maslow's hierarchy, the need for safety, represents a stability layer where companies seek established clients and/or suppliers in the market. Understanding the negotiator's context and overlooking commercial offers in favor of long-term partnerships is crucial. Negotiators exhibit more flexible and open body language, seeking options that enable an agreement, as long as the counterpart is representative in the industry.

The third need in Maslow's hierarchy, the need for belongingness, represents a growth layer where companies are in the expansion process and engage in agreements associated with growth. Negotiators in this scenario display anxious body language, offering attractive negotiations to close deals. In negotiations with suppliers, using growth as an argument for better commercial conditions is common. When companies in the third layer intersect, agreements should be promoted.

The fourth need in Maslow's hierarchy, the need for esteem, represents a reputation layer, where established companies or those with strong principles and values seek brand recognition. In this process, commercial relationships and agreements are defined based on prerequisites related to how the company wants to be perceived in the market. Negotiators exhibit presumptuous body language, associating offers with a purpose. In this layer, the closing process is slower, and counterparts need to align with established partnership assumptions.

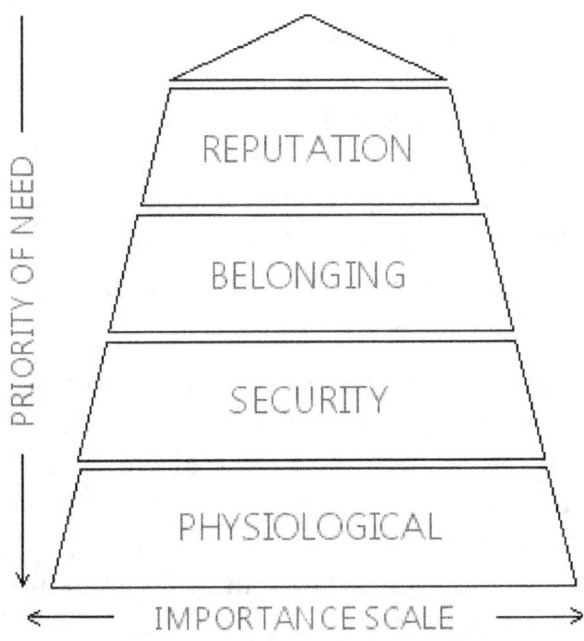

In a commercial negotiation, even though the focus is on agreements, it's important to understand the broader context. The notion of motivation and counterpart deprivation defines how the negotiation will be established and can be understood through the negotiators' body language. The theory of motivation suggests that companies, composed of individuals, have an innate need to avoid pain and seek pleasure. Emotional reading in commercial negotiations is a crucial foundation for assertive communication. Effective communication activates motivation and the desire to achieve the goal. Motivation is highlighted by deprivation (pain). Fear is a sentiment associated with the negotiation process from the initial offer to the closing. There's motivation when the counterpart perceives they might lose a deal to a competitor, just as there's motivation to close a new contract with a new client. In addition to corporate motivation, there's personal motivation that interacts with internal recognition. Successful agreements strengthen individual motivation, where the effort level to conclude a negotiation is amplified by the expectation of reward.

Body language seeks to understand the counterpart's motivation, associating relevant aspects that shape the negotiation. The contexts of deprivation and needs, representing pain and pleasure, interact with various feelings that can be explored through body posture, tone of voice, and micro facial expressions. Body language tunes into momentum, which defines motivation and awakens interest in an agreement. It's important to understand the counterpart's commercial boundaries without forcing a situation that might motivate them to leave the negotiation table. Correlating fear, frustration, and happiness with the options presented at the negotiation table allows for calibration towards an agreement. The options should be logical and challenging, ensuring effective communication. For instance, when facing a lower market offer, it's possible to challenge current suppliers to reduce prices, but body language will suggest a tendency towards calibration.

In companies focused on survival and security, rational options involving business risk are defensively received. Body language translates into body shrinking, hunched shoulders, closed legs and arms, physical barriers, and greater distance, indicating expected reactions. The fear of losing business manifests through evasive looks and trembling hands. Discomfort and distrust towards the outcome are noticeable. In the reading of fear's body language, under commercial pressure, accelerated breathing, abrupt movements, and an energetic tone can be observed. This happens because adrenaline prepares the individual to "fight." In extreme commercial pressure situations, within the context of survival and security, red eyes and dilated pupils might be noticed. No matter how rational the arguments are, the counterpart is emotionally involved, and the negotiation needs to ease emotional conditions to seek a "win-win" agreement.

In companies striving for belonging and esteem, commercial options not aligned with the counterpart's goals are met with frustration.

However, negotiators representing companies in such situations maintain a positive attitude and will seek situations that enable an agreement. Body language conveys tranquility, with an open posture and eye contact. As there's no commercial pressure, gentle and comfortable gestures indicate motivation to achieve an agreement, even if the initial offer isn't suitable. However, if there's no progress, frustration should prevail. Frustration prepares the individual for "flight," and impatience takes over the negotiation. A closed facial expression, a hesitant look, and tense posture demonstrate that the counterpart has lost motivation to seek an agreement. This intensifies with deep sighs and a defensive posture, like crossing arms. A negotiation where the counterpart is frustrated won't lead anywhere. Therefore, paying attention to body language and resuming effective communication is important. In this case, listening and understanding the counterpart's options, seeking to calibrate options to meet specific needs, and bringing back motivation to the negotiation table is crucial.

A human being comprehends a rational environment when avoiding fear and seeking pleasure are not being exploited by the other party. 'Win-win' becomes possible when arguments are supported by logical conditions. In business negotiations, it is common for one of the parties not to be prepared for a closing, making the negotiation superficial. This can lead to postures of fear when threats are articulated, postures of pleasure when force is used for a 'win-lose' proposal, and postures of frustration when the time invested in the negotiation is perceived as useless.

In business negotiation, body language that displays fear, pleasure, or frustration needs to be recalibrated. Rational arguments are the most effective way to bring balance and moderation to a negotiation. However, upon realizing that even in the face of logical facts, the counterpart displays emotional behaviors, it is important to review the communication and how viewpoints are being conveyed.

Summer Redstone, CEO of Viacom, a media conglomerate owner of MTV, needed cash flow to acquire Paramount. Blockbuster was an ideal option, but negotiation with John Antioco was necessary. He was known as an emotional and fair negotiator, using a 'win-win' approach, as long as negotiations aligned with his expectations. The negotiation reported by Summer was filled with emotional highs. Antioco would leave the meeting room seemingly frustrated and pretend to wait for the elevator without even pressing the button. Summer realized this was an emotional tactic, indicating that what had already been offered was acceptable, and Antioco's emotional tactics aimed to boost the deal. Closing a meeting without a logical reason, exhaustively reviewing initial agreed-upon points, and creating a sense of urgency that the agreement could be canceled bring frustration. Summer needed to interpret the counterpart's movements to adapt to the outcome without getting emotionally involved. Patience and inflexibility toward the initial proposal transferred emotional pressure to Antioco, who found himself in a position to close the deal or lose the commercial opportunity proposed by Viacom. In 1994, both reached an $8.4 billion agreement, boosting Viacom's cash flow, which had the sole goal of acquiring Paramount, a goal achieved three months later.

Frustration, when not well emotionally managed, turns into anger, and can even lead to incidents like what happened in the Ukrainian parliament, where argumentation was replaced by punches and kicks. Similarly, in hostage situations, the frustration of reaching an agreement often results in shock operations. In business negotiations, frustration frequently leads to premature closure and the search for alternatives.

It was John Dollard who proposed a theory of frustration-aggression in 1939, suggesting that unsatisfied desires trigger negative emotions. As a result, interpersonal conflicts, such as refusal to cooperate and inflexible attitudes, manifest in body language.

Negotiators constantly need to deal with frustration. In this context, communication and conflict resolution skills are essential to adapt to the dynamics of trade, avoiding pitfalls that lead to aggressive behaviors and ineffective negotiations. Dollard's theory suggests that understanding the expectations placed on outcomes and comparing them with realistic and achievable results is fundamental. Another author who complemented Dollard's theory was the Canadian administrator Victor Vroom. He focused on the expectancy-value theory, combining the outcome with individually assigned value and the effort expended to achieve it.

Frustration has connections to the theories of Maslow and Hull, even though they did not delve deeply into this aspect. When seeking a reward driven by deprivation or needs, there is a direct correlation with expectations at the moment effort is invested. Frustration is amplified when expectations are very high and the result falls short. For example, Viacom could have missed the opportunity to acquire Paramount if Blockbuster had been inflexible. Similarly, the Ukrainian parliament would not have escalated to physical confrontations if expectations had been better calibrated.

The cooperation established by the 'win-win' fallacy is irrelevant in the cases mentioned above. Viacom was solely interested in Paramount, with Blockbuster acting as a facilitator for the agreement. Blockbuster was facing recurring losses, making an agreement that strengthened the brand attractive. In the case of Ukrainian opposition parliamentarians, their interest was a free country, without evidence of Russian military presence on their territory. However, pro-Russia parliamentarians needed to defend Russia's interests, especially considering that the Black Sea represented Russia's only maritime route to the world.

Frustration driven by irrational expectations shapes behavior and organizational culture. Negotiators who understand motivation based on expected outcomes can link emotional conditions to a specific agreement. The size of the reward can encourage more effort from the counterpart, generating higher expectations. When these expectations are not met, frustration arises. Frustration is a natural emotional response that emerges when a person's expectations are not met. It results from a specific event or an unattained goal, often triggering significant losses. Emotional reactions like anger, sadness, disappointment, and hopelessness are associated with the theory of justice, which posits that people evaluate the distribution of resources and rewards based on criteria of fairness and equity.

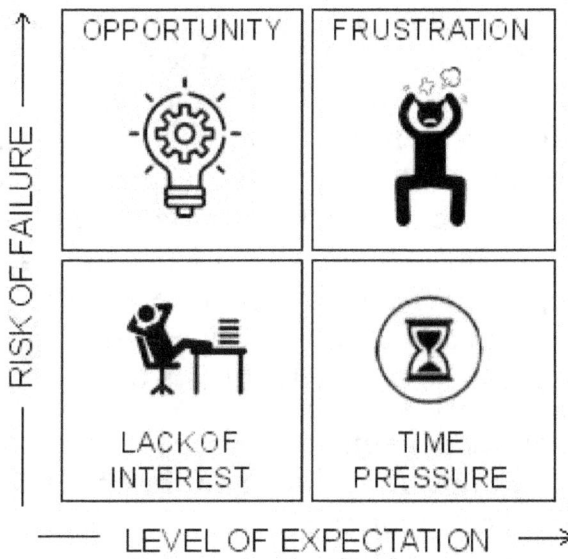

In corporate negotiations, a negotiator deals with

internal and external expectations when interacting with clients or suppliers, as well as with the board and decision-makers. Experiencing a state of frustration is common, and it is rational to regain composure in this emotional state.

Addressing frustrations in challenging negotiations involves anticipating the expectations of both the external counterpart and internal decision-makers. Consequently, promoting open communication, showcasing positions of deprivation and needs, as well as the potential for rewards, ensures a more assertive understanding of a specific agreement. When rationalizing actions and outcomes isn't straightforward, procrastination is triggered as a means of avoiding unexpected results. Emotional dissatisfaction among decision-makers who struggle to rationalize negotiations renders the process unproductive and demotivating. The negotiator needs to grasp the outcome, taking into account deprivation, necessity, and rewards for the business. By rationalizing outcomes, emotional discussions are sidestepped, focusing attention on how to present results without sparking emotional reactions from both internal and external counterparts.

Communication doesn't thrive solely through reports or presentations of outcomes to the board. While it may appear coherent, this isn't how Albert Mehrabian understood effective communication. According to Mehrabian, 55% of effective communication's impact lies within the interlocutor's body language. For instance, during the 2021 Euro Cup, following the match between Portugal and Hungary, Cristiano Ronaldo removed the Coca-Cola bottles in front of him during a press conference and declared "water." This action, lasting less than 10 seconds, cast a negative light on the brand, resulting in media and social media backlash. Consequently, the Euro Cup sponsor experienced tension and discomfort. Cristiano Ronaldo employed nonverbal communication by removing the Coca-Cola bottles from his vicinity and uttering "water." This gesture led to a $4 billion market value loss for Coca-Cola due to stock sales.

Body language and intonation play pivotal roles in communication aimed at converging negotiations into results. Mehrabian's model affirms that communication isn't confined to words but encompasses actions, especially intonation and body language. According to Albert Mehrabian, the 7-38-55 model outlines three principal elements for ensuring assertive communication: the first element pertains to words (7%), the second element involves tone of voice (38%), and the third element encompasses body language (55%). A negotiator should formulate arguments and propose options utilizing the Mehrabian model, thus communicating with confidence where posture and intonation are taken into consideration. Specific body language becomes evident, such as an erect posture, sustained eye contact, controlled gestures, composed facial expressions, and dominance of the space utilized. Engaging in negotiation with a confident individual entails having personal space respected while experiencing both a sense of welcome and intimidation. Body language should be accompanied by suitable intonation, characterized by a steady tone of voice, measured speech, fitting volume, and controlled emphasis, ultimately making negotiations enjoyable and confident.

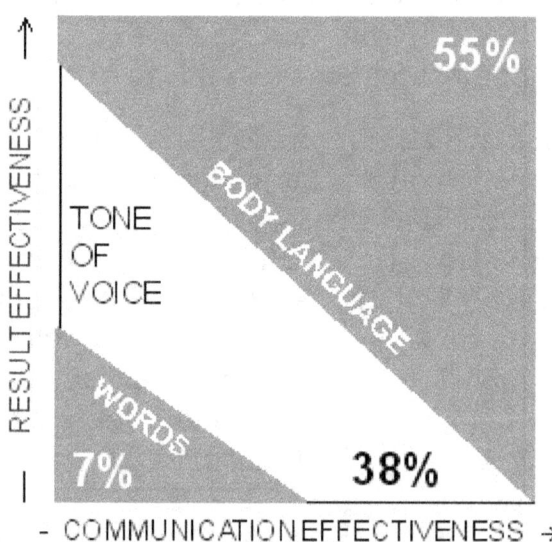

In 2018, the Brazilian soccer team was eliminated by Belgium with a score of 2-1 in the quarter-finals, which marked a negative event for the Brazilian side. However, during the press conference, coach Tite communicated with the media with an upright posture, focused gaze, and a firm tone of voice. His narrative centered around building a strong team for

2022, and the message, coupled with his confident body language and assured tone, instilled hope in the fans. Tite incorporated into his communication strategy the concepts of resilience, learning from mistakes, and preparation. While the message was straightforward, it was the nonverbal communication that provided comfort. The outcome of this press conference secured Tite another four years as the team's coach.

When nonverbal communication is not perceived or trained, PowerPoint slides won't suffice to capture the counterpart's interest. In a 'win-win' communication scenario, both parties establish an environment of trust and respect. Genuine smiles, subtle mirroring, leaning forward, and an open posture, along with a calm and friendly tone of voice, strategic pauses, positive words, and validation that they are on the right track—all of these are noticeable. The negotiation process shifts when dealing with a 'win-lose' situation. If you find yourself in the disadvantaged position, discomfort is evident. The counterpart might push for a 'win-win' closure, but avoids eye contact, suddenly changes posture, repeatedly touches the face, exhibits excessive and uncoordinated gestures, speaks robotically, and has a shaky voice with hesitations in responses. Clearly, the counterpart's nonverbal communication mirrors their body language and tone of voice.

By incorporating nonverbal communication and tone into the context of negotiation, considering deprivations and rewards, attributing emotions like fear, pleasure, and anger arising from constructed needs and expectations, the emotional state must be acknowledged and managed. Rationalizing emotions helps understand the progress of a negotiation. In fear-dominated situations, it's essential to develop options that place both parties in coherent conditions. If pleasure is the predominant sentiment, it's important to assess whether the counterpart feels pressured by a specific agreement. Nonverbal communication offers clues that allow anticipating bluffs and dishonest actions. Presented options should put the negotiation in a state of emotional balance, avoiding frustration due to false expectations. Motivation from both sides must be kept alive, so understanding needs and deprivations is crucial, and options should be crafted considering these aspects in correlation with effort and assigned reward.

Cooperating brings emotional advantages to better perceive the environment, as options aim for fair outcomes. However, fair options can be distorted at the negotiation table by the counterpart resorting to force for a 'win-lose' agreement. At this point, frustration shouldn't prevail; reason needs to dominate, understanding that preparation bolsters the position and can reverse the situation with coherent arguments, accompanied by a confident demeanor and tone.

The emotional influence that affects nonverbal

language in a negotiation is related to the interaction between the unconscious and the conscious. It was Sigmund Freud who addressed primary emotions and human consciousness. According to Freud, any human being is susceptible to being influenced by primary emotions when they do not develop conscious skills while interacting with the external environment. Primary emotions are unconscious and controlled by the ID, representing impulses, instincts, and organic desires, activated by the cerebral amygdala. Impulsiveness is controlled by consciousness, regulated by the prefrontal cortex, and defined by Freud as instances of the ego and superego. Instances of consciousness carry values learned in society and individual perceptions of the external environment. Individuals with consciousness can control speech and actions, even under great pressure from the ID, thus constructing personality.

The ego plays a relevant role in mediating impulsiveness, and even when there is exposure of body language, it's possible to adapt to impulsiveness when the conscious construction that affects the individual's personality is well developed. The ego doesn't act alone and relies on the superego to establish moral standards, censorship, and the entire moral burden attributed to a set of beliefs defined by society and human relationships. The constant communication between the ID, ego, and superego in a commercial negotiation allows for the association of fear and pleasure with consciousness, determining whether the body will show reactions or seek self-control. For example, an individual might fear public speaking but have the ability not to display the ID's pressure due to the ego's skill in adjusting behavior to society, which translates into reputation.

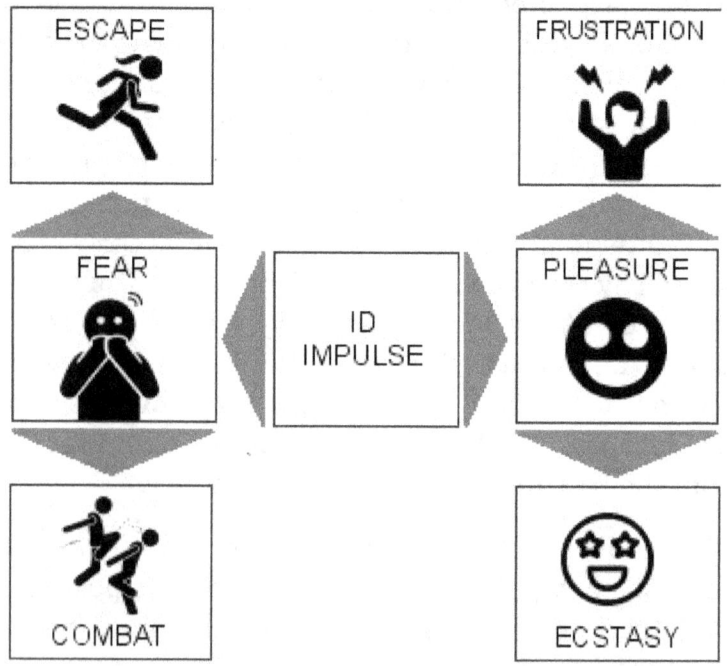

In the analysis of nonverbal language, it's possible to identify behavioral patterns determined by the inefficiency or inexperience of the ego and superego in dealing with the ID's impulsiveness. A negotiator might lie and believe the other party didn't notice, but when lying, hormones are activated to deal with the fear of being discovered. This can trigger unconscious primitive movements, preparing the individual for fight or flight, such as sweating, clenched fists, dilated pupils, and accelerated heartbeats. The superego determines when speech and actions are at odds, even with conscious and skillful ego control, it's possible that in escape situations, the superego reinforces resilient behavior to stay firm or reveals deceptive attitudes.

In the impulsiveness of anger, caused by frustration over a high-expectation agreement and deprivation, the ID, ego, and superego will influence how a negotiator will react to the other party. This can range from uncontrolled aggressive reactions to total emotional control, accompanied by cordiality. However, the amygdala processes anger and only doesn't take disproportionate proportions because the ego and superego assist the individual in conscious interaction with the environment. Sigmund Freud's psychoanalysis enables the development of skills that minimize pronounced nonverbal communication. For this, experience, conscious reflection, and training for possible emotional reactions can prevent a negotiator, even under impulsiveness, from displaying incongruent behavior, thus making external reading difficult. A negotiator's ability guides actions through the integration of the ID with the ego, based on values and principles determined by the alter ego. A personality aligned with moral values determines long-term relationships, trust, and transparency, minimizing irrationality and manipulation.

Human beings create their own emotional precepts, seeking to rationalize a new situation, which causes anxiety. Anxiety can be classified as realistic, neurotic, and moral, which, regardless of logical foundation, brings about a chain emotional reaction and defines counteraction actions. In 1939, the United States launched the "Manhattan Project" upon confirming Nazi advances in atomic bomb technology. Realistic anxiety about a Nazi turnaround in the war under the dominion of atomic technology led the U.S. to invest unprecedented capital, bringing together the brightest minds in science, such as Hungarians Edward Teller and John von Neumann, Italian Emilio Segrè, Polish Emilio Segrè, and Americans Richard Feynman and Hans Bethe, led by Robert Oppenheimer. However, the development of the atomic bomb brought about neurotic anxiety when it became necessary, in possession of the technology, to demonstrate military power to adversaries. American leaders at the time decided to end World War II through inhumane emotional proportions when they determined the dropping of two atomic bombs on Japan, rationalized with the intention that Hiroshima and Nagasaki, two densely populated cities, be destroyed, defining the "loss aversion" to deter further attacks if Japan did not surrender. The atomic bombs immediately killed more than 150,000 people and marked the end of World War II on August 9, 1945

[Chapter 2] Irrationality

"The most extreme form of irrationality is the complete denial of what you dislike."

(Noam Chomsky)

Ricardo Semler and Nick Swinmurn are entrepreneurs with a similar approach to authority, although they never had a professional or personal relationship. Ricardo is a Brazilian entrepreneur who revolutionized Semco when he introduced unconventional approaches to rescue the company from bankruptcy. According to Semler, active employee participation in decisions ensured more assertiveness and maintained engagement for the best agreements. Nick, an American entrepreneur, also revolutionized Zappos with a horizontal organizational approach, where negotiations empowered employees for agreements, building engagement and focus on optimal outcomes. Authority plays a significant role in negotiation because no matter how skilled a negotiator is, when approval from a superior is required, the 'win-win' takes on a different dimension. Proficiency in nonverbal communication and preparation for negotiation becomes futile in a vertically hierarchical scenario, capable of deeming 'win-win' agreements as unacceptable. Horizontal companies rationalize expectations, allowing for quicker decision-making, progressing and sharing negotiation outcomes, not for approval but for a second perspective. A negotiator must grasp how decisions are made on their side of the table and the counterpart's side. The more top-down the decision-making, the more irrational the agreement is expected to be and the lower the engagement. Motivation takes different forms that need to be understood for an agreement to be fully accepted.

The influence of hierarchy on decision-making is explained psychologically, where orders and expectations from authorities have significant effects on human behavior, even overriding personal and moral convictions. Stanley Milgram was a psychologist who evaluated authority in obedience experiments. One such experiment revealed alarming conclusions: participants were instructed to administer electric shocks to a 'learner' when answering questions incorrectly posed by the 'teacher.' Both the 'learner' and 'teacher' were actors, and the electric shocks were fake; the figure of authority was represented by the 'teacher.' The teacher would ask a question, and if the learner answered incorrectly, the participant was authorized by the teacher to administer shocks to the learner, with the shocks increasing after each round of questions. Milgram concluded that most participants would continue to administer shocks even when the learner showed distress, as long as the teacher assumed responsibility for the shocks administered. Hierarchical organizational structures influence decisions, especially when figures of authority define processes where negotiation results must be approved. When the authority figure accesses and alters negotiation outcomes, a condition of obedience is present.

However, authority doesn't solely carry a negative connotation in negotiation outcomes. Leaders can leverage positions and results without impacting the negotiator's autonomy. Stewart Clegg, an English sociologist, demonstrated that those with greater power and status make riskier decisions and are less sensitive to others' perspectives, confirming that hierarchy promotes overconfidence and resistance to opinion changes. Stewart reveals that results can be improved when an authority actively participates in closures. Nevertheless, Serge Moscovici, a Romanian psychologist based in France, investigated how social position in the hierarchy affects the ability to achieve favorable outcomes. Serge confirmed that higher hierarchy holds more power and is more successful in negotiations where the counterpart holds a lower hierarchical position. For instance, a manager negotiating with a director tends to concede and accept concessions more readily than someone with a similar or lower position. Lastly, Richard Daft, an organizational theorist, introduced an interesting aspect when evaluating how organizational hierarchical structure affects decisions, with horizontal structures being quicker and more collaborative than vertical ones.

Authority brings irrationality to negotiations when there is a divergence in approach with the negotiator. Abrupt changes in agreements can be observed when a vertical hierarchy takes control of the decision-making process. It is crucial to understand how a negotiated business agreement will be concluded. To achieve this, knowing the hierarchical structure, decision-making flow, and organizational culture allows for anticipating irrationality and building relevant strategies. The more hierarchical the decision, the slower and potentially more irrational it may become. Some companies use hierarchy as a tactic to delay price increase agreements and to add extra conditions after an agreement seemingly had been closed. When a pattern of irrationality in changes to previously established agreements is noticed, the influence of authority becomes evident. This results in negative effects on outcomes, possible emotional frustration, procrastination in defining and achieving important progress, as well as leading the negotiating representative to have low motivation due to a lack of autonomy over a commercial agreement.

When facing a situation in which the counterpart lacks decision-making autonomy and established agreements change due to internal authority influence, it characterizes a 'win-lose' scenario. In this context, it's important to rationalize the process and use this situation to reevaluate the loss situation. In organizations where decision-making centralization is more present at the higher hierarchical level, it's relevant to schedule the final negotiation step in a meeting where decision-makers are present. Seeking a 'win-win' scenario with the high-level management representative isn't ideal since changes in the agreement can occur. In vertical models, one may find demotivated representatives who don't pursue 'win-win' agreements, either due to inadequate preparation or a lack of understanding of high leadership expectations. In this scenario, dedicating time to negotiation to understand how decisions are made is more valuable than trying to make options flexible that aren't understood by the negotiator. There's a risk in pursuing a 'win-win' scenario when procrastination in decision-making becomes evident. In this case, it's appropriate to work with a 'win-lose' approach, forcing the decision-making meeting with high leadership, including creating a sense of urgency and setting deadlines for the final agreement.

In companies with a horizontal approach, the dynamic is different from authoritarian models, considering that the negotiator is also a decision-maker. In this environment, the focus on 'win-win' becomes relevant, and irrationality is more controllable since it originates from the individual.

It's expected that in horizontal organizations, negotiations are based on principles, fundamentals, parameters, and metrics that guide internal decisions. Thus, the negotiator understands the limits of a 'win-win' agreement. Horizontal companies tend to establish decision-making processes that provide negotiators with autonomy. Understanding how decision parameters are defined ensures assertiveness, and even in the face of irrationality, it's possible to reverse the situation given an understanding of the decision-making process.

Irrationality, whether in vertical or horizontal companies, manifests through the behavior of the negotiator or representative. The motivations for an agreement and nonverbal communication provide clues on how an agreement will progress. Injecting a sense of urgency activates emotional conditions, as it defines a sense of loss when decisions aren't made. Irrationality is understood when verbal communication distorts what was perceived in negotiations, both verbally and nonverbally. The negotiation's context underpins needs and expectations. However, even when the negotiation converges to previously aligned points, there isn't always a resolution. Faced with irrationality, feelings of frustration are common as the decision-making premises aren't understood. However, irrationality can be a negotiation strategy that tests the counterpart's reaction and decision-making regarding sought changes. Dissembling in challenging negotiations is dangerous and detrimental to commercial relationships and negotiation progress. However, in situations where irrationality and dissembling are protected by the counterpart's power, a 'win-lose' approach is expected to conclude the negotiation. In this case, the negotiation takes on a more strategic, long-term focus.

An example is the acquisition of Time Warner by AOL in 2000, through a merger process. AOL had gained a prominent position with the advent and growth of the internet. AOL's motivation to become a reference in entertainment and media coincided with the opportunity to acquire the conglomerate Warner Bros, HBO, and CNN. AOL paid $164 billion to be incorporated in the AOL Time Warner merger, a value considered misaligned with market conditions and ultra-optimistic future valuation estimates. AOL was so interested in Time Warner that its premises, values, and forecasts made sense to AOL's leadership, even though it was irrational from the perspective of market analysts. The merger ended up being a failure, exacerbated by the 2000 internet bubble and the cultural divergence between the companies.

In 2001, PepsiCo acquired Quaker Oats in an acquisition process. Fearing Coca-Cola's dominance in the sports beverage market, PepsiCo initiated emergency negotiations with Quaker to acquire Gatorade and other products. PepsiCo and Quaker agreed on a $13.8 billion deal in negotiations that lasted less than a year. The acquisition of Quaker Oats made sense to PepsiCo's leadership given the competition and market expectations. However, it was evaluated as an irrational position driven by loss aversion. The executives' concern about losing market share made the Quaker Oats acquisition coherent due to the exclusive need for Gatorade in the portfolio. The Quaker acquisition later proved to be a financial failure due to integration difficulties and a high acquisition price, resulting in losses and investor criticism.

Irrationality is attributed to emotional and psychological factors, leading individuals to rationalize decisions motivated by factors devoid of reason. Dan Ariely, a behavioral psychologist, conducted a series of experiments that demonstrated irrationality in decision-making. Ariely confirmed that people make decisions against their own interests, defying reason. He showed that expectations, emotions, social norms, and external influences affect how we make economic decisions. Among Ariely's experiments, "loss aversion" and the "zero-cost effect" are particularly relevant in business negotiations. The "loss aversion" experiments demonstrate that people have a stronger aversion to loss than attraction to gain, resulting in irrationality when facing loss conditions. The "value anchoring" experiments show that people distort the value of something when exposed to an arbitrary reference, leading to irrationality in the valuation of offered products or services.

In the "loss aversion" experiments, Ariely demonstrated irrationality in various experiments, some of which were quite interesting. For instance, in the "free coffee" experiment, participants are offered a free cup of coffee or a discount voucher. Group 1 must choose between free coffee or nothing, group 2 must choose a discount voucher or nothing, and group 3 serves as the control/reference group. The results showed that group 1 valued consuming more coffee than group 2 due to the loss aversion to missing the opportunity for free coffee. Another experiment is the "fictional stock market," where participants hypothetically invest in a company's stocks, which initially drop by 50% and then recover to the purchase price. Participants are offered the option to sell or keep the stocks. The majority chose to sell to recover their money, indicating that the negative experience of the initial loss influenced the decision. Another experiment is the "movie popcorn," where groups receive different buckets of fresh and stale popcorn. Group 1 receives a large bucket of fresh popcorn, group 2 receives a medium bucket of fresh popcorn, and group 3 receives a medium bucket of stale popcorn. The results showed that group 3 consumed more popcorn than groups 1 and 2—a behavior driven by loss aversion, where people strive to consume more stale popcorn to emotionally recover a hypothetical value. In groups 1 and 2, since the popcorn was fresh, there was no sense of loss, and hence no need to exert effort to consume more.

Loss aversion puts individuals in an emotional state that leads them to seek psychological conditions that bring a sense of gain. In the "free coffee" scenario, people accept coffee even when they don't want it, simply because they don't want to miss out on something free. In the "fictional stock market," people sold stocks without making a profit because they didn't want to experience the previous loss again. In the "movie popcorn" experiment, people consumed something undesirable to emotionally recover a hypothetical value. "Loss aversion" is an irrational impulse that impacts negotiators and corporations in making emotional decisions in business negotiations.

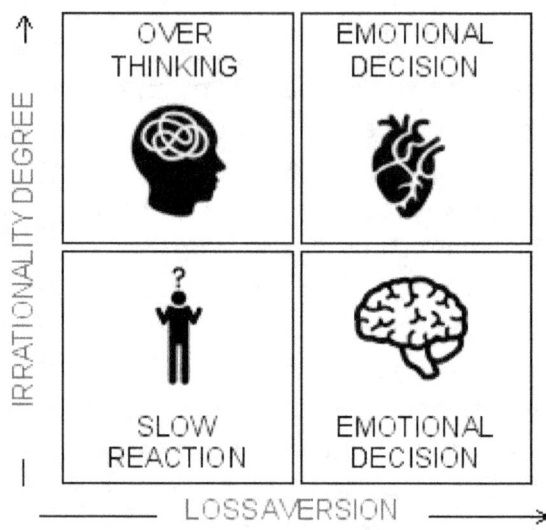

In the 'anchoring of value' experiment, irrationality was demonstrated by Ariely in experiments like the 'wine price' experiment, where two options of wines for purchase were presented: one with a normal price and another with an inflated price. However, the wines were identical. People would taste the wines and assign scores to their quality. The results showed that the majority of participants evaluated the wine with the inflated price as having better quality and taste than the wine with the normal price. This demonstrated irrational perceptions influenced by a monetary value. Another experiment is the 'CEO salaries', where participants were asked how much they thought CEOs of large companies should earn as annual salaries. However, before giving an answer, Group 1 was exposed to a high salary reference, while Group 2 received a relatively lower reference.

The results showed that people, when exposed to a reference value, tended to estimate salaries close to the presented value.

Anchoring of value puts the individual in an emotional state that leads them to make decisions based on references provided by others. People rationalize and believe their decision is correct, even if it isn't. Rationalizing emotion is dangerous, as it complicates understanding the situation and hinders changing the initially deposited belief. In the 'wine price' experiment, people anchored to a higher price label will struggle to admit that the taste and quality do not differ from the cheaper wine because the price was rationalized into something tangible. The same relationship can be applied to CEO salaries: it's easier to accept the rationalization that a CEO earns $10 million when others around them have similar salaries, which can even cause emotional reflections when reality distorts the rationalization associated with emotional conclusion.

In negotiations, negotiators are prone to irrationality, whether influenced by authority or external influences, as well as by the rationalization of emotions influenced or manipulated by third parties. Defining principles and preparing help avoid irrationality, but it's also important to be mindful of how the counterpart acts, avoiding emotional traps. Emotion is a set of electrical impulses and hormones activated by the amygdalae; it's a complex process to understand when a decision is being manipulated or influenced, as the motivation caused by emotional stimuli doesn't consider reason. In difficult negotiations, the counterpart may position themselves with arguments of loss and present distorted references to influence your analysis. When realizing that an agreement triggers emotional conditions, where fear or pleasure take control at a certain moment, it's always important to take a step back and review the established negotiation process.

An action or the potential for action is physiologically formed in our brain through synapses. Emotions are processed as electrical impulses and transmitted by neurons, being released and defining the synapses. A synapse is created when a person smiles, even when feeling sad. In this way, the brain needs to create synapses that allow muscles to move in order to produce a false image of happiness. Irrationality becomes dangerous when the rationalization of an emotion that corresponds to irrational behavior is justified with logic.

Rationalizing emotions is a defense mechanism that enables dealing with complex feelings. However, this damages human behavior when synapses are strongly built. Rationalizing emotions leads to the suppression of genuine feelings, which accumulate and cause psychological stress. When internal feelings and external behaviors that are not cohesive adapt in a synapse, false authenticity and confusion in interpersonal relationships occur.

Rationalized emotions in an irrational way affect decision-making, as they disregard reason, since they focus on concealing feelings. The problem with rationalizing feelings incorrectly, such as smiling in moments of sadness, brings internal tension and deceptive behavior. This triggers anxiety and defines synapses that hinder discernment in decisions. In chapter five, objective ways of dealing with logical facts and limiting emotions in a decision-making process will be addressed.

Carlos Mauricio Furtado

[Chapter 3] Influence and Manipulation

"When you realize you're being manipulated, you're already on the path to freedom."

(Vernon Howard)

In the 1920s, Charles Ponzi introduced a method that promised returns of 50% within 45 days through the purchase and resale of international postal coupons. Charles rationalized his method by claiming that price discrepancies between postal coupons from different countries enabled extraordinary returns. Ponzi's method made sense to those who invested their money, and miraculously, their investments would increase by 50% after 45 days, confirming the efficiency of the proposed method. However, the coupon method was nothing more than a fraudulent investment scheme, involving paying returns with money obtained from new investors. The Ponzi scheme, characterized as a pyramid, doesn't generate legitimate profits and always relies on new participants to sustain itself. Therefore, old investors were rewarded when new investors deposited their money in hopes of astronomical returns. This process of manipulation is still observed and, astonishingly, continues to yield results due to human greed and emotional conditions.

The pyramid model is a crime but illustrates how susceptible people are to manipulation. A recent case was Bernie Madoff, who operated one of the largest and most famous Ponzi schemes in history between 1990 and 2008. Madoff managed to attract wealthy and intelligent investors with rhetoric promising returns consistently better than market performance. However, in 2008, the scheme came to light after the financial crisis, and Madoff was discovered and sentenced to 150 years in prison. Ponzi schemes are recurring and leverage emotional triggers such as social pressure, a sense of urgency, and aversion to loss. Con artists gain trust when promises are fulfilled, creating a self-reinforcing belief.

Manipulation and influence walk a fine line, differing in the intention of the influencer. Influencers seek a "win-win" situation, while manipulators acknowledge the existence of a "win-lose" outcome. Influence is based on ethical and moral principles. Even in cases of "win-lose," the winner adheres to morally recognized principles, as in cases of war, independence, and rights. Manipulation involves understanding emotional triggers that influence people toward self-benefit, as practiced by Ponzi and Madoff. Influence aims for cooperative and equitable outcomes, guided by fair standards. Notable examples include Gandhi, Martin Luther King, and Nelson Mandela.

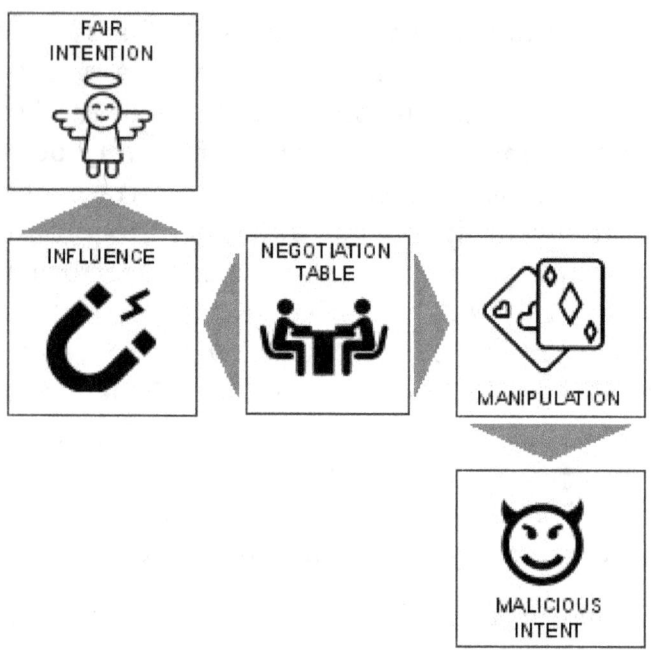

In negotiations, manipulation and influence don't necessarily occur at the negotiation table but behind the scenes. Sellers and buyers try to sway decisions, presenting arguments and using behavioral effects that trigger emotions and provide influence. Humans will always be influenced in commercial negotiations as part of the flexibility process. However, it's crucial to identify whether manipulation is present and if decisions won't lead to a dead end.

The seven deadly sins categorize when influence or manipulation is applied. In the 4th century, Pope Gregory I codified manipulation into sins based on vices and behavioral tendencies. This book isn't religious in nature, but Gregory I's approach was ingenious, despite the absence of scientific methodologies. The first sin is vanity, corresponding to excessive arrogance and superiority over others. The second sin is greed, representing excessive craving for material goods and wealth. The third sin is lust, characterized by excessive sexual desires. The fourth sin is envy, defined by the desire to possess something that belongs to others. The fifth sin is gluttony, focusing on excessive food or drink consumption. The sixth sin is wrath, where uncontrolled anger takes over the individual. The seventh sin is sloth, related to lack of diligence and negligence of duties and responsibilities. In negotiations, when it's unclear whether you're being influenced, evaluate through Gregory I's perspective and determine if the offer doesn't exaggerate in any way.

A negotiation isn't just a conversation in a meeting room where motivations, needs, and offers are discussed. A negotiation takes place behind the scenes, in the surroundings and external environment; the meeting is a formalization of what's already happening in practice. India achieved its independence on August 15, 1947. The negotiations were conducted between representatives of the British government and Indian leaders, with Pandit Nehru being prominent. The negotiation tactics involved influence and popular pressure, led by Mahatma Gandhi. Without Gandhi's ability to influence and mobilize the population, Nehru likely wouldn't have succeeded. Winston Churchill led the British Empire and aimed to resist independence as much as possible. However, the persistence, resilience, and determination of the Indian people weakened the sovereignty of the British Empire, already weakened by World War II and no longer under Churchill's command. Nehru's negotiations for an agreement were influenced by nonviolent actions, respect, and compassion. Approaches of disobedience, like strikes, marches, and boycotts, exerted pressure and influence on the British concerning demands for independence.

Influence involves persuading the counterpart beyond the negotiation table, influencing the rationalization of emotional discomforts that drive an agreement. Influence is a powerful tool and, when perceived positively, it's inspiring, motivating, and encouraging. Manipulation, on the other hand, refers to influencing deceptively, with the goal of obtaining individual advantages. Manipulation distorts information and employs emotional triggers to deceive the counterpart. Influence or manipulation occur simultaneously with negotiations, through arguments that support consequences. A negotiator can use the company's reputation, its values, the proposal, and market position to influence suppliers and customers. Influence takes on more advanced proportions than just a commercial offer. However, a negotiator can also manipulate suppliers and partners, abusing their power to manipulate the negotiation, claiming potential losses greater than those proposed in the agreement.

Skilled negotiators establish principles for a negotiation, understanding external influences, power dynamics, and potential concessions. Negotiation sets motivations but also limits for an agreement, where a "win-win" is achieved when parties seek transparency, cooperation, and flexibility to adapt the proposal and progress towards an agreement. Inflexible approaches are irrational and hinder an agreement, and influence, combined with deprivation and rewards, can enable a self-centered and inflexible stance to be shaped more rationally.

Defining principles in a negotiation follows guidelines related to expectations and values. Initially, own goals and interests are defined, understanding priorities and limitations. Then, the counterpart's position is highlighted, reflecting on differences. Subsequently, the focus shifts to common interests, enabling cooperation. Lastly, and most importantly, differences are acknowledged, forcing the parties to dedicate time and energy to finding the best common ground or, when feasible, ending the negotiation. Gandhi and Churchill, despite sharing common principles of fighting against oppression, democracy, and freedom, diverged on the hegemony of the UK, being an inflexible point for Churchill, who needed to resort to popular influence.

Carlos Mauricio Furtado

Difficult negotiations must be thought out both inside and outside the negotiation table, especially when divergences obscure the counterpart's stance. The focus is on seeking solutions for discrepancies, where emotional tactics of influence attempt to flexibilize the counterpart's positions through empathy and active listening.

Emotional tactics of influence cannot be mistaken for manipulation, no matter how good the intentions of a negotiator may be. Goebbels manipulated the German population, taking advantage of the emotionally weakened conditions of a post-war society. The Nazi Party used manipulation to secure popular support and elect Hitler. Goebbels' communication featured grand and dramatic images, enthusiastic crowds, impressive military parades, and Hitler's fiery speeches. The aim was to create a powerful and charismatic image of the party's leader, highlighting unity, strength, and greatness. Cinematic techniques and assertive editing contributed to an atmosphere of reverence and admiration, promoting Nazi ideals and thus manipulating the German population. The thin line between manipulation and influence is always separated by self-benefit. The rhetoric of "win-win" without evident mutual benefits is possibly manipulation and needs to be reversed. Manipulation will always exploit emotions, masking the true intentions of the counterpart.

In manipulation, misinformation is an effective tactic, diverting attention from rational facts and distorting reality, exploiting the vulnerability of the counterpart. Manipulators force disproportionate agreements when they perceive dependence and aversion to loss. For instance, a supplier might manipulate a price increase when they perceive that a disproportionate loss of revenue might occur if a specific product isn't made available. They might create manipulative rational arguments, avoiding mentioning the link between cost increment and revenue loss.

In influence, transparency and values access the conditions of an agreement. Arguments provide confirmation and rationality, focusing on mutual understanding. Influence seeks social proof, referencing decisions based on the approval of others. Therefore, negotiating with an individual without external references from third-party opinions makes influence less effective.

The Uber business model required regulatory approval in various countries to function. Negotiations were difficult as taxi drivers organized protests and strikes, causing chaos in cities in order to manipulate regulatory decisions. Uber's technology brought convenience to users, transparent pricing, flexible employment opportunities for the population, ensuring passenger safety, fair prices, and a more balanced economy. As there was a market confrontation where inevitably taxi drivers would lose, the "win-win" focus shifted towards the population. Uber wouldn't succeed if it tried to understand taxi drivers' viewpoints behind closed doors and convince regulators. The power of public opinion was necessary, so it was important to influence the population about the benefits of Uber. Marketing campaigns influenced benefits and educated the population; discounts on rides encouraged users to install, register, and use the service. Political pressure would arise when the system was already operational, and authorities needed to decide whether to cancel it. Uber didn't wait for approval to operate but negotiated the legal continuation of its operation. Uber leveraged the chaos caused by taxi strikes to showcase the system's ease and attract more users to its platform. The rapid growth of the user base strengthened Uber's influence against regulatory authorities. Uber's negotiation didn't happen at a negotiation table but outside of it.

When making decisions, humans utilize two hemispheres of the brain: one is intuitive and quick, and the other is rational and slow. Daniel Kahneman, a psychologist who proved through experiments how people process decisions and how they often incur irrationality due to the cognitive convenience of using the intuitive (fast) hemisphere. Kahneman's confirmations show how people can be easily influenced or manipulated when they persist in using intuition. An experiment called the "panic effect" gathered a group of participants and showed them a video of a person falling into a cold-water pool, asking them to evaluate how unpleasant the situation was. Then, a task was defined in which each participant could choose an immediate amount or a larger amount later. The results showed that participants who watched the video and reported discomfort were more likely to choose the immediate money, suggesting that emotions influence decision-making. Another experiment called the "confirmation bias effect" involved describing a fictional person to a group of people. Participants received two descriptions: the first was of an introverted and shy person, and the second was of an extroverted and confident person. The results showed that they chose the option that confirmed their beliefs about their own personality, suggesting that we are influenced to opt for what is familiar and similar to us. A third experiment called the "endowment effect" allowed the option of selling a mug, with one group physically receiving the mug and another group not. The results showed that people value what they already have, with most people in the group that had the mug preferring not to sell, while the opposite happened with the other group; suggesting an attachment to physical items. A fourth experiment called "focused planning" asked participants to imagine in detail the gain of a voucher for a fancy dinner. Then, two dinner options were offered: the first, a gourmet dinner at a fancy restaurant; the second, a simple meal at a family restaurant. The results proved that most opted for the family restaurant, suggesting that imagining detailed planning for the fancy dinner built disproportionate expectations, making the option of the family restaurant more attractive and secure.

Kahneman's experiments bring important reflections on behavior and how our brain absorbs information and decides, being more relevant that in most cases, we opt for emotional and intuitive decisions, without any rationality. In negotiations, we are susceptible to making quick decisions, suggesting an emotional approach based on intuition. Quick decisions suggest the use of the intuitive hemisphere, an entry channel for influence and manipulation. However, there is the rational hemisphere that processes information more slowly but considers more information, principles, and coherence. Rational decisions require energy, are slow and deliberative, forcing a diversion of the brain to faster and automatic processing, which can lead to rationalizing an emotion. Negotiators need to standardize analysis and rationalize business offers; the reflective ability assesses scenarios, consequences, and informed options for an agreement.

Understanding that the rational process is slow and exhausting confirms that there will be a diversion of the brain to intuitive associations, which demands that companies create decision-making processes. Two examples mentioned by Kahneman show a biased diversion to the fast hemisphere. The first example, called the "confirmation bias," asks you to assert that all prime numbers are odd; then, they present examples of prime numbers like 3, 5, 7, 11, 13... and ask people to find a even number. In this example, people quickly convince themselves that there is no even number among primes, neglecting the number two. Another example is called the "availability heuristic," where people are asked to estimate the probability of a plane and car accident. Plane accidents are emotionally striking and are usually overestimated; to have an answer, there is a plane crash for every 81 million flights. A final example of diversion is the "cognitive problem of the bat and the ball," in this mathematical example, it is said that the ball and the bat together cost $1.10 and that the bat costs $1.00 more than the ball; then, the cost of the ball is asked. In this example, our intuitive system anticipates the result that the ball costs $0.10, but the correct answer is $0.05.

Negotiations are recurrently influenced by emotions; only experienced and skilled negotiators manage to sidestep the cognitive trap and make assertive decisions based on rational information processing. It's common to notice counterparts utilizing the intuitive hemisphere or attempting to emotionally persuade you. The "availability bias" is one of the most used approaches and consists of recreating recent events, leading the counterpart to evaluate decisions based on immediate available options. For example, negotiators dealing with a series of increases will be more susceptible to accepting a new increase without assessing its validity. The "confirmation bias" approach is also often seen, presenting only arguments that confirm a position. For instance, a seller requesting a price increase by arguing energy and raw material costs, while the buyer presents an argument about increased volume and an improved economic scenario. Each side presents strong yet superficial arguments. However, due to cognitive fatigue, the parties seek an intermediate and acceptable solution. The availability and confirmation biases suggest that there is still much room for improvement in negotiations since quick approaches tend to lead to detrimental decisions for the business, possibly resulting in a "win-win" situation where there is clearly a loser.

Influence and manipulation in negotiations are powerful techniques to guide counterparts into accepting an agreement that serves one's own goals and objectives. In commercial approaches, sellers and buyers have specific goals that provide productivity to companies. While the seller seeks revenue and profit, the buyer seeks reductions. Two common influence and manipulation approaches in negotiations between sellers and buyers are the "loss aversion" and "reward motivation." The former exploits the fear of missing out on an opportunity, while the latter taps into the pleasure of having effort adequately rewarded. Negotiators aim to engage the counterpart in an approach that highlights advantages and consequences in a specific negotiation. This influences the counterpart's attention and engagement in pursuing an agreement. However, influence loses its grip when manipulation is perceived—whether it's understanding that the loss is not real or that there won't be a significant reward after the effort expended.

"Loss aversion" was observed in mobile communication technology in 2012. Facebook noticed a sharp decline in the use of Messenger in developing countries like Brazil, Mexico, India, and Indonesia. They realized a rival with high leveraging potential in terms of simplicity, convenience, and free features of text, voice, and video messages. Due to this "loss aversion" to a technology that was better received by users, Mark Zuckerberg offered $1 billion in cash to the founder of WhatsApp, Jan Koum. Jan perceived the proposal as manipulative and declined, given WhatsApp's potential and exponential growth. The "loss aversion" was greater on Facebook's side, which needed to take a position to mitigate this aversion. Facebook acted swiftly, recognizing that the loss of users would be detrimental to the business. They increased the offer to $4 billion in cash and $12 billion in stocks, formalizing it as their final proposal. This put the "risk aversion" on WhatsApp's side, which had to decide between risking competition with Messenger or accepting Mark Zuckerberg's last offer. In February 2014, Jan Koum accepted Facebook's offer.

"Motivation by reward" was observed in 2010 when NASA was seeking partnerships to reduce its dependence on Russian technology. However, NASA needed a competitive supply and opened a bidding process for the "Commercial Crew" project, intending to approve private companies if they could offer a more economical option than the Russian Soyuz spacecraft. The reward was a $2.6 billion contract for multiple launches. NASA's investment in the Russian spacecraft was about $80 million, which motivated American companies to offer a cost-effective solution, benefiting from a 30% cost reduction. SpaceX was low on funds and saw NASA's reward as motivation to provide a suitable solution. Elon Musk personally led the negotiations with NASA and the development of the Falcon 9, a reusable rocket that not only ensured the company's survival but also made SpaceX visible to the world and prominent in aerospace projects worldwide.

Influence and manipulation use mental triggers and psychological tactics that put the counterpart on alert. The leadership of Facebook and PepsiCo was influenced by situations that triggered specific mental triggers, such as the "anticipation" trigger when Facebook acquired WhatsApp and the "sense of urgency" trigger when PepsiCo acquired Quaker as Coca-Cola launched Powerade. Triggers are specific and circumstantial; note that Pepsi activated the emergency button only with Coca-Cola, even though Quaker had been operating in this market for years, and Facebook only took action when it saw a mass migration of users in India and Brazil in its reports.

Mental triggers influence negotiations and outcomes by providing anxiety and human emotional reactions. In 2016, Cambridge Analytica was hired to assist in the presidential race, and the consultancy's methods to promote the image of a future president became a scandal, alerting to mass manipulation through social media via "fake news." Cambridge could detail psychographic profiles and map the personality of a potential voter community. With technology, it could differentiate political propaganda and calibrate relevant emotional triggers that would make people spread false information and change the opinion of the masses. Cambridge Analytica succeeded in its mass manipulation plan but faced retaliation and consequences from government authorities, leading to the company's bankruptcy in 2018. Manipulative practices were exposed to the world and showed how easily humans on a large scale can be influenced through mental triggers and technology. Triggers of fear, authority, scarcity, reciprocity, social validation, empathy, compassion, and anger were employed in fake news with the exclusive focus of winning votes.

In marketing, the use of mental triggers to influence consumers, though questionable, is commonly seen in advertisements. People are attracted to triggers that create anxiety and stimulate consumption. In challenging business negotiations, mental triggers are commonly used, and some of them have practical efficiency. The first mental trigger is "urgency," which puts the counterpart on alert and anxious for a quick decision when offers require a rapid decision with the consequence of loss. The second mental trigger is "scarcity," which activates emotional mechanisms that deepen aversion to loss if the agreement is perceived as a unique opportunity to become part of a select priority group. The third mental trigger is "authority," where leadership endorses the opportunity, providing expectations that create pressure for execution. The fourth trigger is "anticipation," where the presented opportunity is associated as unique and prioritized, and it will be made available to the market later. This trigger is effective when there is competition for the same supplier or customer. The fifth mental trigger is "exclusivity," where a unique opportunity is defined exclusively for the counterpart, bringing strategic preference and attention.

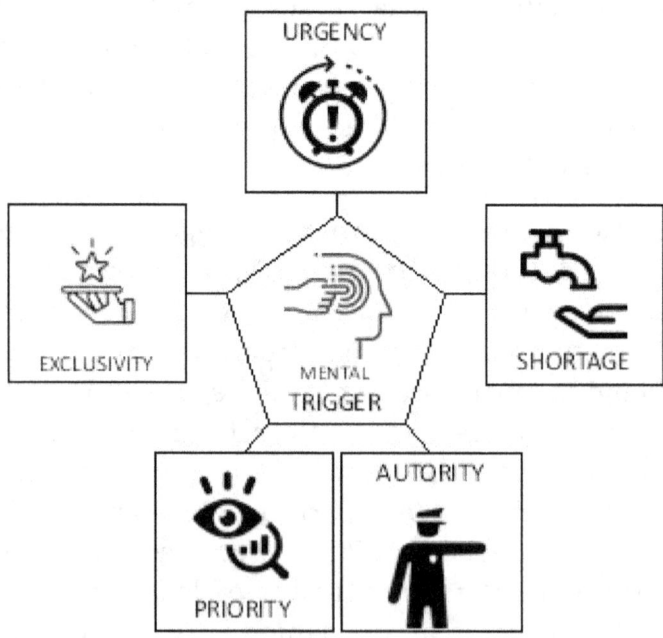

In 2010, Spotify initiated negotiations with record labels due to its revolutionary streaming technology, which aimed to reduce the impact of piracy at the time. Spotify's business model required access to music but also offered free access to users. Daniel Ek needed to convince record labels, such as Sony Music, that Spotify was sustainable and that authorizing distribution rights would reduce piracy. For record labels, the idea of combating piracy through free access seemed manipulative, leading to natural resistance to the proposed agreement.

Spotify used negotiation techniques that anchored record labels with an initial low offer for copyright rights, with flexibility to negotiate gradual increases. Spotify's goal was to establish partnerships with record labels and make decision-makers aware of the value of streaming. This resulted in counteroffers and concessions that made the negotiation possible. The triggers of "anchoring" and "scarcity" triggered emotional conditions that led the parties to rationalize the relationship between music, piracy, streaming technology, and the strategic partnership with Spotify.

Record labels saw value in associating with Spotify, provided it was a partnership and not just a copyright concession. Anchoring is an influencing technique that has an emotional component and can be rationalized. In negotiations, anchoring is often used to set the parameters. Depending on the context, starting with an offer of 10 to reach 8 or starting with

1 to reach 2 can be applied. The "win-win" approach loses effectiveness when the first offer is perceived as manipulative, requiring a fresh start.

Negotiations typically start from the specific interests of one of the parties, which defines emotional and technical approaches. Putting the first offer at a better value than expected sets an anchor that the counterpart needs to contest. In manipulation, the offer is irrationalized to evoke emotional triggers, while in influence, logic is applied, but there is an interest in maximizing results, but within realistic limits.

In 2006, Disney acquired Pixar in a negotiation with Steve Jobs, who used the "loss aversion" technique when positioning the initial offer. Pixar was attractive to Disney due to its developed computer animation technology and successes like Toy Story and Monsters, Inc., which justified the acquisition. Jobs' initial offer was anchored at $7 billion, allowing concessions with each counteroffer and resulting in a deal of $6 billion and 7.5% of Disney's shares, totaling $7.4 billion.

In 1974, Daniel Kahneman and Amos Tversky conducted behavioral studies that demonstrated the power of anchoring, revealing that people base their decisions on references. This highlights the importance of the first offer in the final outcome. "Anchoring" sets the conditions for an agreement, which can involve prices, deadlines, and other additional elements.

Robert Cialdini offers relevant insights into anchoring in influence and highlights the choice of the anchor as crucial in influencing the counterpart. Cialdini suggests that the more plausible the anchor, the higher the chance of success, indicating a persuasive and non-arbitrary anchor. He proposes three anchoring approaches: the "anchor close to the intended agreement" introduces an offer slightly better than desired, creating an anchor that influences decision-making. The "contextual anchor" presents an offer in a context that makes it more attractive, leveraging favorable perceptions of the offer. The "concession anchor" presents a high initial offer and then flexibly makes concessions, inducing the counterpart to accept a more advantageous offer.

Anchoring is widely used in negotiations due to its emotional appeal and influence on the counterpart. This allows for the identification of decision-making behavioral patterns and the pursuit of agreements that align with mutual understanding of a "win-win." However, the use of anchoring can appear manipulative, especially when forcing the counterpart to make minimal moves in the offer, which can result in commercial conflicts. Using anchoring requires rational justification to set limits and positioning. Recognizing influencing strategies that exploit mental triggers, anchoring, and emotional induction helps anticipate successful negotiations.

[Parte 2] The Power of Reason

"Reason is the only faculty capable of making us understand true and useful things."

René Descartes

In 1969, Neil Armstrong and Buzz Aldrin were part of the Apollo 11 mission. NASA's objective was to achieve the position of the first country to set foot on the Moon. Irrationality took hold of a portion of the population who preferred to believe in theories lacking logical and scientific foundation, relying on misunderstandings, misinterpretations, or misinformation. While the irrational side manipulated people with the theory of the filming studio, where the Moon was supposedly filmed in Hollywood, with recognizable issues such as shadows, clinging to the atmosphere and wind, the absence of stars, and the solar radiation on the Moon that would burn the photographic film, the rational side was based on convictions supported by scientific aspects and evidence.

Reason could associate relevant aspects, such as live broadcasts and videos showing the lunar walk and astronauts collecting samples and conducting experiments, as well as the participation of thousands of witnesses, including scientists and NASA employees directly involved in the mission, who attested to its authenticity. Recognizing that the US had forged and convinced so many people to lie just to claim they were the first to land on the Moon sounded irrational.

In other contexts, as with the man's landing on the Moon, logic can take two paths: incoherence and coherence. In negotiations, it's common to see one of the parties clinging to irrelevant facts and using them to become inflexible. Emotional negotiators are difficult to handle in the emotional sphere when reason fails to persuade them; however, it is expected that reason will guide a reasonable negotiation and allow for the construction of suitable scenarios for both parties.

Reason refers to the human capacity to think, analyze, evaluate, and make decisions. Logic and the construction of evidence build reasoning and critical thinking, enabling one to act impartially and objectively. In business negotiations, reason offers limitless possibilities to develop arguments and seek solutions that underpin an agreement. Through reason, it is possible to understand needs and interests in depth, including emotional aspects. Data and information become relevant ammunition; thus, statistical argumentation and an understanding of the market, finances, and logic ensure that data translate into expectations and results.

Without reason, negotiations lose focus, and it is common for one of the parties to engage in deception. Reason allows for the definition of clear objectives and the foundation of all aspects raised, from creative options to situations where there is no justification for the continuation of an agreement. The absence of reason places the parties in rigid positions, as they cannot go beyond the felt emotion. Therefore, reason brings adaptability when something deviates from the expected, enabling the reconfiguration of proposals, criteria, premises, concessions, and risks without losing respectful form and efficient communication.

[Chapter 4] Logic and Critical Thinking

"Logic isn't everything, but logic is the only thing that allows us to distinguish between the things that make sense and the things that don't make sense."

(Immanuel Kant)

In 2018, Nestlé and Starbucks announced a partnership that expanded the presence of their brands in packaged coffee. Starbucks held a strong position in cafes, while Nestlé had a global distribution and coffee production at scale. The companies logically joined forces to maximize product availability and mutual growth. Starbucks would leverage its products in supermarkets, and Nestlé would diversify its coffee portfolio with a valued brand.

Financial analyses alone do not define a decision; logic plays an important role as it complements premises through criteria. Logic is structured reasoning that validates conclusions based on available information. In commercial negotiations, when coupled with logical arguments and reasoning, it enables sound decision-making and helps avoid emotional manipulation. Logic separates itself from emotional approaches, making it easier to construct alternatives and coherence for an agreement. A logical flow identifies objectives, gathers information, analyzes options, evaluates scenarios, and validates premises, with critical thinking acting as a barrier against irrationality.

The concept of logic originates from philosophy, with Greek influence, particularly from Aristotle and his structuring of thoughts and arguments. Mathematics elevated logic to another level, shaping the digitized world we currently live in. George Boole was significant in the application of mathematical logic and the introduction of the concepts of "1" and "0" for electronic and computational processing. Boolean algebra associates "false" and "true" in complex computational processes that simulate human logical thinking, such as artificial intelligence. "True," represented by the digit "1," and "false," represented by the digit "0," when associated with logical functions like "AND," "OR," and "NOT," have limitless applications that can be used in negotiations in any circumstance.

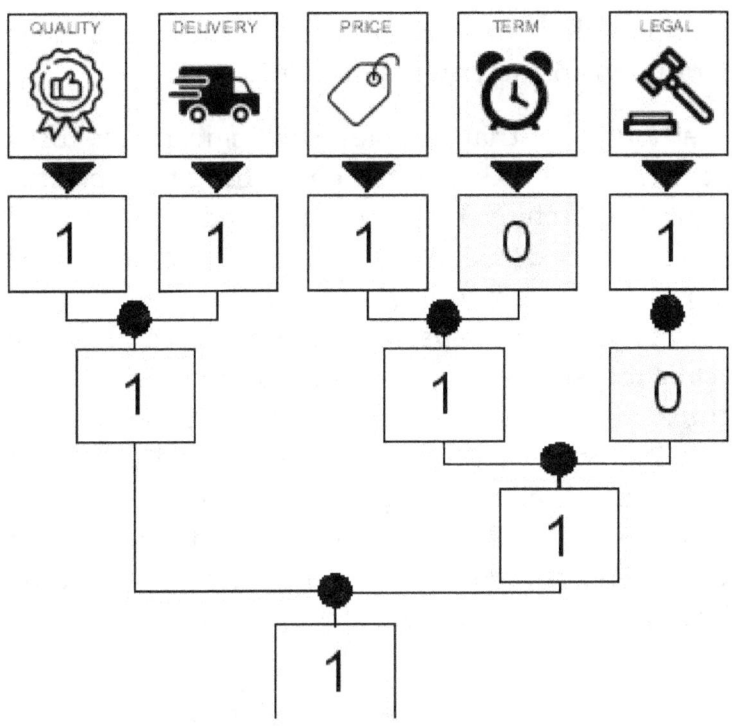

The objective of a negotiation is to reach an agreement, with "YES" and "NO" serving as the logical representation of the criteria and conditions presented. Negotiations combine premises, definitions, and agreements that make up the final decision. A premise can be a price below expectations and a deadline equal to or longer than expected, with the combination of these two premises associated with a logical "AND" function serving as the reference for making a decision. Boolean logic deals with binary outcomes and enables limitless premises and criteria, but simplifying communication and adapting relevant premises is what makes an agreement possible.

A methodology that enables the logical flow of a negotiation is SMART, where combining the Specific, Measurable, Achievable, Relevant, and Time-bound aspects allows decisions to communicate efficiently towards an agreement. SMART starts with the goal (S), specifying the expected outcome. The objective must be measurable (M), defining completion criteria. It must also be achievable (A), avoiding an always false criterion. In negotiations, the more criteria there are, the more challenging it becomes to reach an agreement. Therefore, it is necessary to define the relevance (R) of each criterion and, finally, determine a timeframe (T) for the conclusion of the negotiation.

Negotiations without criteria are not logical and rely on emotional conditions and a sole focus on the final result. Logic identifies criteria that can lead to binary outcomes ("YES" and "NO"), and based on these criteria, it models the structure of the negotiation, defining all possible outcomes based on the established premises and criteria. Logical negotiation allows for flexibility, associating requests and expectations in a sequence of "YES" and "NO" oriented toward an agreement. The definition of relevance helps identify limiting criteria for a final agreement and allows for specific action. A negotiator can request a cost reduction from a supplier, defining a goal aligned with market premises, commodities, and productivity, setting a 3% reduction as the target. All arguments and preparations are based on meeting this criterion to reach an agreement. The process is designed to understand how to obtain a "YES" from the supplier, even considering new premises and requested criteria. Logic aims not to freeze a model but to allow flexibility and understanding of how a final agreement can be achieved.

The logical model is assembled for each negotiation, making all related premises and associations defining criteria that enable argument analysis for progress evident. The agreement, when considering both parties' premises, is a "win-win" scenario. However, logic can be built for one's benefit. Logical reflection analyzes contradictions and paradoxes, defining degrees of truth and falsehood. This analysis enables arguments to be constructed more effectively, avoiding emotional conflicts. It is essential to consider flexible negotiations, where the logical model is redesigned with new premises and criteria, potentially leading the argument down a different path but never losing track of what was initially addressed, safeguarding against deception and manipulation.

Amazon purchased WholeFoods from hundreds of purchasing options. The company establishes a logical process before any price or agreement negotiation. Initial criteria are set to determine whether the allocation of negotiators is necessary or if the opportunity should simply be terminated. The preliminary criteria that need to be met are actually three. The first is confirmation that the business has market potential. The second is whether the business is financially viable, and the third is whether the business aligns with the company's strategy. Negotiations need to be justified and aligned with a higher purpose. Negotiating prices and conditions cannot precede basic, non-negotiable criteria. Identifying the opportunity is more relevant than negotiating the best commercial terms for a business that does not make sense. Coca-Cola does not negotiate the purchase of LinkedIn because a negotiator invested time and effort to secure a good price. It simply does not make logical sense.

At the commercial negotiation table, there are buyers and sellers, each with criteria defined based on different perspectives. Logical reflection on commercial demands, their relevance to the counterparty's business, potential counterattacks, the consequences of a disagreement, and even emotional involvement can be anticipated when using a logical approach model. Negotiating skills reflect the negotiator's ability to develop a logical model and adapt it based on new information, assumptions, and contexts. The adaptation and complexity of assumptions and criteria allow for predicting result scenarios and understanding restrictions without clinging to irrelevant but emotionally influential conditions. A supplier may claim that the offer is the last and that they will sell to another, but if there is a criterion that does not justify the agreement, the "loss aversion" trigger will not be activated.

In 2003, Liz challenged the logical sense of the medical and scientific community by proposing the "Edison" technology, which could detect medical conditions such as diabetes, cancer, and cardiovascular diseases from a drop of blood. Even in inconsistent circumstances, Elizabeth Holmes founded Theranos, standing out for rhetoric that lacked evidence of the technology's effectiveness and functioning. Nevertheless, she managed to negotiate capital investments with experienced investors like Rupert Murdoch and the DeVos family, as well as establish partnerships with pharmacies, medical centers, and obtain attractive conditions of price and terms from medical supplies suppliers. In a short time, Theranos was valued at $9 billion, which led to investigations by more skeptical and logical negotiators regarding the presented technology, its risks to patients, and the reliability of tests. The FDA audited Theranos, identified diagnostic fraud, and ordered the prohibition of blood tests conducted by the company. In 2018, the company declared bankruptcy, and in 2023, Elizabeth Holmes was sentenced to prison.

Logic is not used in negotiations to validate an agreement or to determine if a threat or opportunity is true. In both Amazon's case, which establishes preliminary criteria to decide whether it's worth negotiating the purchase of a new company, and for the clients, investors, and suppliers of Theranos, there should have been criteria for accepting key partnerships. Irrationality seeks valid logical arguments to justify a position, so a "bluff" can be effective when the counterparty is emotionally involved, and logical models are incomplete. Negotiators often use assumptions and criteria that, if not verified, end up being accepted as true without ever being questioned.

A "bluff" can be countered through "reverse logic," in which logic is inverted in search of coherence regarding the consequences attributed to the "bluff." If a seller offers a unique deal, claiming that everyone else is buying and bluffs by saying this is the only option for you to decide, you can logically evaluate the truth of this statement in reverse. Reverse logic assumes that the proposed agreement, based on the emotional arguments of the counterparty, is a "bluff." In this case, obstacles that would make the "bluff" unsuccessful are evaluated, creating scenarios that allow reflecting on the validity and consequences if the "bluff" is recognized as true or false. Note that all scenarios consider the agreement as true, but a premise about the truth of the bluff is added, creating criteria that allow reflecting on four possible extreme outcomes.

Charlie Munger is a partner at Berkshire Hathaway and often emphasizes his ability in reverse logic as the reason for his financial success in shareholder meetings. Munger simplifies the approach, arguing that it is more coherent to identify an undesirable outcome and rationalize the traps that lead to that result. For Munger, focusing on avoiding errors and pitfalls is the formula for success in negotiations and decisions, where exhaustive reflection on failures is more effective than assuming that a plan will succeed. Munger's formula is applicable in a "bluff" situation as it can reverse positions by recognizing the motivations that would lead the counterparty to make a bluff, thus allowing an assessment of which situations would make the counterparty withdraw the bluff from the table or which new assumptions could be included in the agreement to render the potential bluff irrelevant.

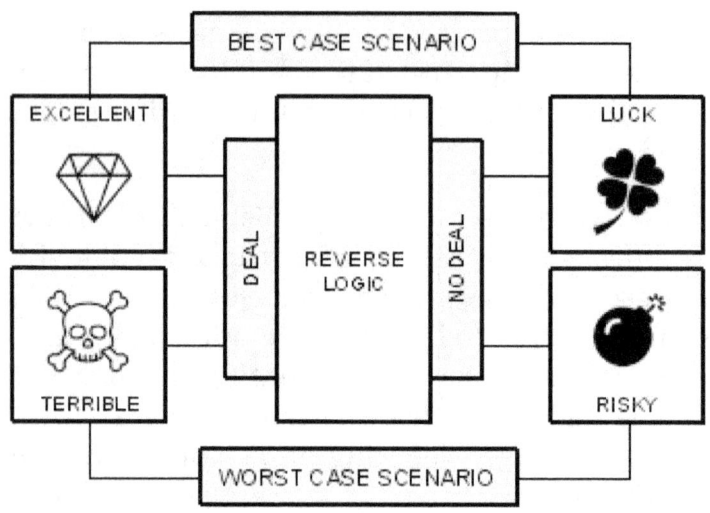

In 2019, Walmart didn't bluff when it approached its entire supplier chain with specific criteria for increasing efficiency and reducing costs. Walmart's arguments were that prices needed to be more competitive for customers, and the company needed to improve its financial position compared to competitors. Negotiators acknowledged the possibility of widespread frustration but also knew that renegotiating contracts, redefining volumes, and favoring suppliers suitable for the efficiency policy could reverse what seemed like a negative approach. Walmart provided purchasing volume premises, which put suppliers in a delicate position since losing Walmart's account would require a tremendous effort to replace. On the other hand, Walmart's negotiators were prepared for reactions from some suppliers and would treat commercial negotiations as exceptions. Walmart's logical approach, which set a specific goal, gained the attention of suppliers on a large scale and prompted them to reconsider the continuity of a client the size of Walmart. If they didn't accept, they would prepare a consistent argument that would flexibly adjust an agreement without incurring a supply risk. Walmart was highly successful in this approach; results increased substantially, and stock prices rose significantly during this period. On the other hand, suppliers who adhered to the policy or sought a flexible agreement maintained a significant volume with a bias towards an increase.

In commercial negotiations, logic associates criteria up to resolutions in a BATNA (Best Alternative to a Negotiated Agreement), which is an acronym that stands for the "best alternative to a negotiated agreement." BATNA was proposed by Roger Fisher and William Ury, Harvard professors who attributed negotiations with conflicting interests to a process that identifies options for a less-than-ideal but mutually acceptable agreement. BATNA's approach considers options for an agreement only if the parties are in conflict. For Fisher and Ury, an acceptable worst-case scenario is a "win-win" when the parties force themselves to be flexible and build a parallel scenario that promotes progress. Walmart did not set a unilateral "take it or leave it" policy, but in recognized critical situations, BATNA allows negotiators and suppliers to enter into a mutual agreement different from what was expected.

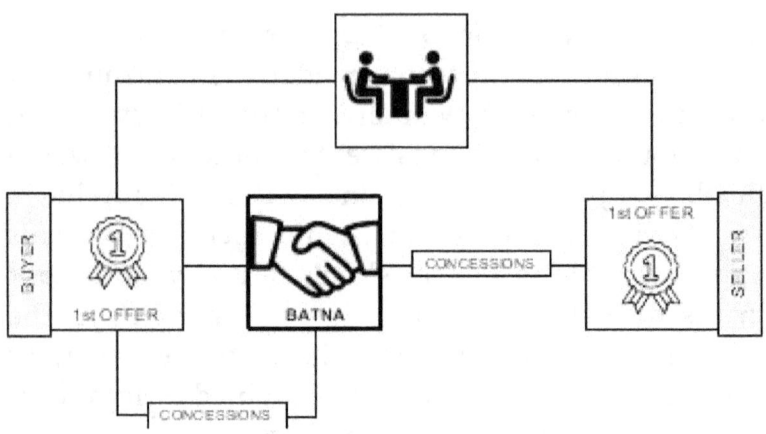

BATNA, when combined with reverse logic, has unlimited possibilities to turn emotional arguments that manipulate a "win-lose" condition from a bluff or the use of force into a rational and reliable process. The approach to the "worst-case" scenarios includes consequences associated with accepting or rejecting an agreement. Reflecting on reverse logic helps in understanding and suggesting options that go beyond expectations but are still advantageous for the business, or at least more advantageous than ending negotiations without any agreement. Hypothetically, a supplier pressures for a +10% increase while the buyer seeks a -10% reduction. The supplier threatens to halt future deliveries, and the buyer threatens to cancel the contract. In reverse logic, negative consequences are assessed, such as the delivery blockade and its impact on the business, and how certain options could be managed without accepting the initial offer. At the same time, the critical path is defined, and options for a BATNA are sought, something between +10% and -10%. The premises and criteria allow for a new positioning argument, sensitizing the counterpart to flexibly adjust the initial offer in a rational environment. On one side of the table, the supplier argues that additional quality costs are unsustainable, while the buyer argues about budget constraints and loss of competitiveness that would affect volume. The "worst-case" scenarios have already been considered, putting the initial offer in an acceptance position. However, threats can extrapolate controllable scenarios, activating triggers associated with loss aversion as an option to draw the attention of vertically integrated companies that promote fair negotiations.

In 2010, Oracle filed a lawsuit against Google, alleging patent infringement. Oracle claimed that Google's Android had copied specific Java APIs' code. Both companies sought to argue their positions to avoid a lengthy legal process. Oracle's motivation was financial, as they had just acquired Sun Microsystems for $7.4 billion, and capitalizing on this investment was crucial due to the success of the Android operating system. On the other hand, Google rejected the claim of intellectual property infringement and refused to pay royalties for what they considered inappropriate. They argued that their use of Java followed the doctrine of "fair use" and that APIs were not subject to copyrights. Java was the foundation of Android's development, unlike Apple's iOS, making the patent infringement claim a delicate issue for Google. While Google could have directed the negotiation towards a reasonable royalty payment, they chose to argue legally because they knew that "fair use" was an exception to the exclusive rights of authors and copyright holders when it was intended to balance the public interest in promoting creativity. Since there were divergent positions and no commercial agreement was reached, both companies had to spend millions on a legal process that lasted over 10 years and reached the United States Supreme Court, which issued the final decision that Google had not infringed patent laws and that the use of APIs was considered "fair use."

In negotiations involving divergent claims and threats, confrontation is required, starting with an opening negotiation. At this stage, flexibility is established by defining positions and proposals between the parties. Reverse logic encompasses concerns, motivations, and possible immediate actions, including the consequences of reaching an agreement. By not accepting the demand to pay royalties, Google left Oracle with the option of investing resources in a legal process. Google had legal support, but they also had the option to reprogram Android or pay royalties to Oracle. In the Oracle vs. Google case, various scenarios could be outlined based on assumptions and criteria.

Clarity regarding the main impacts and the agreement's flexibility allows for exploring reasonable options and arguing with the counterpart about the unfeasibility of an agreement. Google argued that "fair use" was legal and that using Java's monopoly condition would inhibit partnerships and developers' usage. Moreover, public opinion could see Oracle as a monopolistic and restrictive company. Arguments about likely consequences made the counterpart reflect on whether it was worth taking the negotiation to another level or if the effort versus the chance of success justified maintaining the position. In Oracle's case, Google's arguments were not effective, leading both companies to take the case to the highest court.

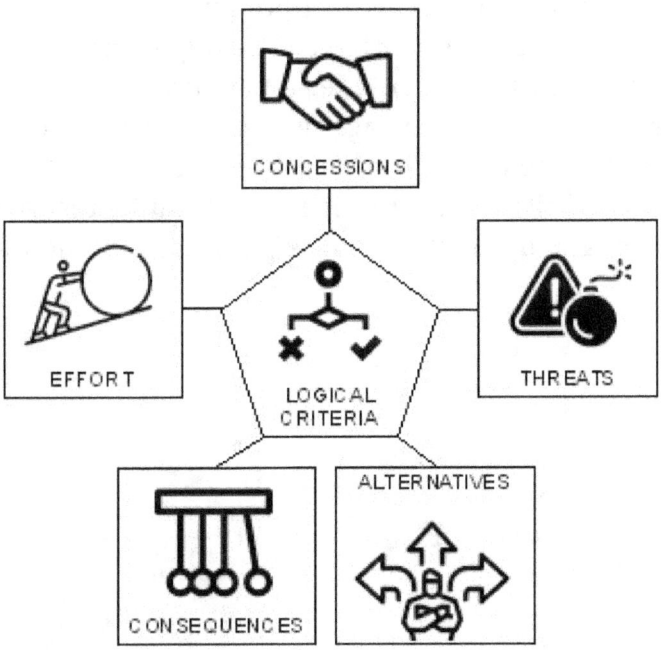

Mapping consequences through reverse logic generates options and explores possible paths to avoid negative consequences. Negotiation must weigh arguments that move the counterpart away from the initial position toward something satisfactory. The focus is on flexibly making concessions through solutions that make the counterpart reassess the consequences and force satisfactory options. In the previous example, where the buyer was pressured by a +10% increase and a -10% reduction, the buyer could be affected by the halt in deliveries, which would harm future sales. With reverse logic, alternative options that eliminate the threat from a specific supplier are evaluated. At the same time, options that maintain deliveries without absorbing the +10% price increase are negotiated. The buyer may agree to review quality criteria, offer a new project, or simply offer a lower percentage while accepting a price increase. The options aim to create a better scenario than the initial one, and it is essential to record the request and understand subsequent developments.

[Chapter 5] Statistics and Probability

"Statistics is the science that tells us what we don't know, using what we know."

(Richard von Mises)

In 2016, Verizon faced a strike involving more than 39,000 workers in the United States. It was crucial to reach an agreement in the negotiations, considering the estimate that each day of strike would result in a revenue loss of $200 million. Strike is a right protected by American legislation and, statistically, it is resolved quickly, as it promotes understanding and agreement between the parties. The initial position of Verizon workers was a salary increase of +6.5%, maintenance of health benefits, and protection against outsourcing. Accepting the initial demand of the workers would put Verizon in a delicate position, mainly because it would compromise decisions and future reactions related to outsourcing. Therefore, Verizon acted quickly and formally offered the union a proposal that focused on the most relevant point for the workers, using it as leverage to flexibly address the other issues. Salary increase was the most relevant and urgent criterion, so Verizon offered a +10.9% raise for a fixed period of four years and confirmed the maintenance of the health plan. However, they sought to maintain outsourcing freedom with the commitment to create 1,400 new jobs during the agreement period. Verizon's counterproposal was accepted, and the strike came to an end. Verizon showed perspicacity in identifying the point of divergence, which was outsourcing, and worked with a counteroffer that improved the salary issue, forcing the union to yield regarding outsourcing. Verizon statistically understood the most relevant criterion and crafted an irresistible counterproposal.

Statistics is a mathematical discipline that interprets data and provides conclusions. The concept of statistics dates back to antiquity, with roots in Babylon and Ancient Egypt. Later on, statistics was strengthened and applied to physics by Moivre, Laplace, and Gauss, and subsequently by other mathematicians such as Fisher, Pearson, Neyman, and Galton. They developed sophisticated models of distributions, regressions, hypotheses, and variances in practical applications. In negotiations, statistics has relevant applications, as it comprehends contexts, behaviors, and markets that influence the positioning of the parties involved and determine the probability of success in an expected scenario. Negotiators and companies that use statistics recognize market and counterpart patterns, enabling the construction of logical approaches based on historical patterns, future expectations, feelings, and associated risks.

The obsession with historical data and the

convenience of accumulating data on a large scale provide incalculable opportunities for corporations and negotiators. In negotiations, the concept of statistical regression allows correlating dependent and independent variables, focusing efforts and attention on relevant premises. Statistics also enables the rational translation of emotions in negotiations through the "sentiment index." In this science, the feelings of the counterpart are quantified and correlated with market sentiments, which is relevant to understand whether the pressure applied is consistent or feigned, thereby anticipating protection against emotional approaches. In negotiations, statistics also allows measuring risks, compressing the negative consequences related to a likely factor. In this case, the negotiator can anticipate results and rationalize areas of risk in disagreement.

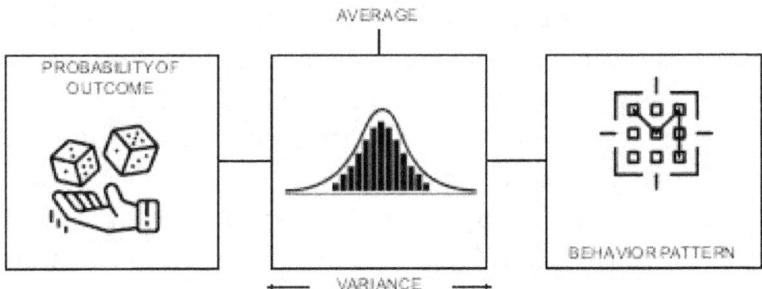

Hedge funds are rational options for corporations that negotiate contracts with suppliers or customers. Hedge funds are statistical oracles that take on future risks with the guarantee of price stability for customers. Negotiators who use statistics employ hedge strategies assertively and devise approaches that anticipate the market. In the market, there are hedge options to protect future contracts, where agricultural producers can safeguard the price of their products, companies can shield their commodity and currency costs, and negotiators can secure their portfolio of customers and suppliers. Statistics comprehend abrupt market fluctuations and foresee future behavior patterns based on past behaviors.

McNuggets is an innovative and iconic product from McDonald's, launched in 1983, consisting of breaded and fried pieces of chicken. McDonald's was hesitant to implement the plan, given the chicken's price variability, which could impact margins and demand if the price were consistently passed on to the end customer. Bridgewater, led by Ray Dalio, proposed a solution that would maintain price stability, satisfying the interests of suppliers and McDonald's. Ray Dalio's insight into the cost of chicken allowed for the construction of statistical models that linked the chicken's growth process to its diet, confirming that cost variation was directly associated with the market value of corn and soybeans. This enabled Bridgewater to ensure the stability of the chicken's price through futures contracts for corn and soybeans. Ray Dalio's negotiation and solution focused on price stability, as futures contracts ensured that chicken producers would receive feed at controlled prices. Consequently, McDonald's could set the price of McNuggets and launch the product globally without worrying about sudden fluctuations in the short term. The agreement between chicken producers and McDonald's was only possible because Ray Dalio understood relevant cost variables, and there was a future market for purchase. McNuggets, along with Big Mac and French fries, represents 60% of McDonald's revenue and demonstrates that negotiations supported by statistics allow price control without speculation, pressure, or short-term surprises.

Predicting commodity prices uses statistical regression, a science that assesses the relevance of associated variables. Commodities are raw materials that can be produced on a large scale without the need for a high level of industrialization. Negotiators who understand commodities related to the traded products and the variables that influence these commodities have advantages in any negotiation. In the negotiation between McDonald's and chicken producers, without an understanding of corn and soybean prices as pricing factors, it is possible to predict a high trade conflict. Producers would likely halt deliveries if the prices of soybeans and corn were not adjusted. This would force chicken producers to seek alternatives, putting emotional pressure on those dependent on McDonald's to operate. Statistical regression and knowledge of chicken costs enable the analysis of corn and soybean price fluctuations to determine whether the McNuggets' price would be attractive and profitable even with abrupt variations. The statistical regression method quantifies a product and relates variables such as inflation, exchange rates, and commodity prices to trends and patterns that allow for evidence-based decision-making, moving away from guesswork. Negotiations supported by statistical data, arguments, positions, and decisions are backed by mathematical models that support expected outcomes. In negotiations where there is no rational basis, the negotiator with more bargaining power influences a "win-lose" outcome. For example, McDonald's could have haphazardly launched McNuggets and still be negotiating and pressuring producers today, driving some to bankruptcy and others to the drastic decision of ceasing supplies. However, McDonald's and the producers decided to adopt a safer approach for both sides, avoiding the inevitable power struggle that would lead to a "win-lose" outcome. Not necessarily every solution involves using hedge and futures contracts; each business will have its specificities, and it is the negotiator's competence to design solutions that provide stability and rationality.

Regression plays a crucial role in negotiations as it allows for the analysis of historical patterns. In the statistical regression analysis, the negotiator begins to examine relevant variables, often used as arguments by suppliers and clients in search of concessions. Understanding these relevant variables enables the prediction of future behaviors. In this scenario, it is feasible to monitor the online market and, based on coefficients, identify trigger points for reactions, both while waiting for a response from the other party and while acting as a negotiator.

During a regression analysis, outliers can occasionally appear, which are data points that deviate from the norm and do not have a direct association with the variables. The negotiator must understand these outliers to identify opportunities or recognize errors. If a negotiator engages in a negotiation without conducting a regression analysis, they risk being caught off guard and experiencing negative emotional consequences.

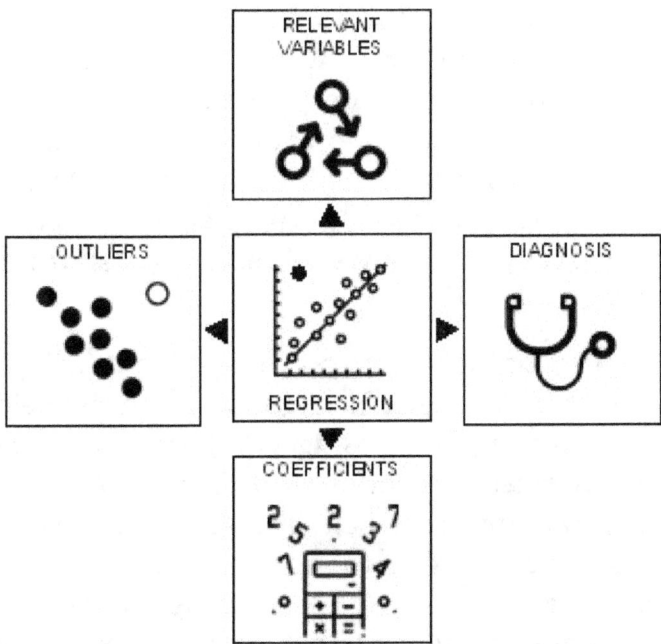

James Harris Simons has been trading futures contracts since 1989. The Medallion fund, from his company Renaissance Technologies, boasts an average annual profitability of 60%. Medallion operates through complex statistical algorithms that analyze the appropriate time to allocate capital. A relevant model for Jim Simons is the "sentiment index," which compiles data from news, social media, and emotional investor perception into statistical patterns correlated with reality, allowing for the definition of momentum. The "sentiment index" mathematically translates qualitative perceptions like joy, sadness, frustration, anger, and other feelings into natural language processing (NLP) computational models. The association of positive, negative, and neutral words is compiled by computational algorithms, which, along with historical data, determine context. Negotiators can use the "sentiment index" to anticipate business approaches and formulate arguments that put the counterpart in a more favorable emotional state for an agreement.

The sentiment index is responsible for measuring the "emotional intensity" of a negotiation. In the field of Natural Language Processing (NLP), sentiments need to be converted into numerical values representing polarity, ranging from negative (-1) to positive (+1), and can also take into account intensity using weights such as -1, -2, -3. The sentiment index serves the purpose of identifying a trend when polarity and intensity are combined. These trends guide the potential tone of a negotiation and assist in the preparation of the negotiator.

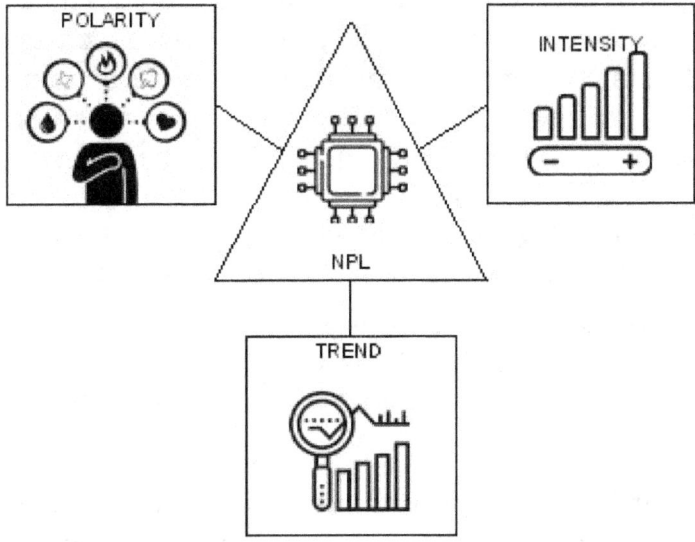

In 2015, Adam Mckay released a film that portrayed crucial moments before the collapse of the US subprime mortgage market in 2008. The movie "The Big Short" showed how investors used statistics differently to determine trading and momentum strategies. Negotiator Michael Burry, a hedge fund manager, used statistics to determine the risk of subprime mortgage defaults, identifying when a significant number of loans were destined to collapse. This conclusion led him to negotiate with banks to purchase insurance called "credit default swaps" (CDS), which would reward him if the US real estate market collapsed. CDS played a significant role in the collapse of banks because they exposed the fragile subprime system. AIG was the largest issuer of CDS, a profitable product because they did not believe in a collapse in the US mortgage market. However, with the disproportionate increase in defaults, the company was forced to pay large sums to fulfill its obligations. This caused insolvency on a large scale and required external funds, triggering a warning and government intervention. Michael Burry's negotiation for the creation of CDS was a "win-lose" model, but it shows how distinct perceptions benefit one party. Burry would never have succeeded in his CDS negotiation if AIG also understood the defaults. In fact, AIG could have avoided an imminent collapse.

"Statistical risk" underpins alertness and organizes the portfolio for risk mitigation. Experienced negotiators diversify their portfolio with suppliers, clients, and assets to minimize collapses. Constant risk analysis and proactive actions that increase variables minimizing risks are professional. Therefore, a negotiation cannot be viewed in isolation, where two parties equal arguments and forces for results understood as the best possible or "win-win." The specific negotiation needs to go hand in hand with the strategy that positions the negotiator in a situation where choices are possible. When a negotiator is dependent on the other party, there is a risk, just like AIG became dependent on CDS. A negotiator represents a company and their own interests, so with each negotiation, it is necessary to review how the whole will be influenced by the outcome of a specific negotiation. It is tempting to receive an irresistible offer from a supplier that will significantly increase the company's profit. Negotiations are not isolated in the corporate world. AIG could have closed a CDS with Michael Burry and not suffered any setbacks if the market collapsed. However, it was the offer of CDS and thousands of policyholders that led to insolvency. The same happens when a seller negotiates large volumes with a large customer and becomes dependent on that business and relationship, or when a buyer neglects other supply options because they believe the current supplier and commercial relationship are advantageous. In any situation where there is dependency, there is the possibility of dominance, which is likely to lead negotiations into emotional spheres. When witnessing a relationship of dependency that could lead to the financial collapse of a particular product, segment, or even the company, agreements and decisions should take risk into account.

Risk is of great importance in the business approach and should be assessed based on the probability of a negative or positive reaction, as well as the sensitivity to deal with a specific variable. Probability involves understanding reactions to specific arguments, ranging from opposing arguments to the decision to leave the negotiation table or even retaliate by canceling the deal.

Arguments that have a high probability of generating

negative reactions should be carefully crafted to ensure that the sensitivity arising from a risky reaction is minimized. Negotiators can use their authority as a means to reduce this sensitivity and can address different issues separately, allowing time for reflection and internal alignment, thereby avoiding highly probable negative emotional reactions.

The "Monte Carlo method" was created by the mathematical geniuses Stanislaw Ulam and John von Neumann. The method involves simulating various random scenarios and estimating possible results. The approach of the "Monte Carlo method" is logical, as it recognizes the problem, quantifies the variables, and calculates results based on sampling and simulations. Monte Carlo is used in negotiations to resolve disputes and identify critical moments. For example, to determine the launch of McNuggets and the selling prices, McDonald's could use a model that varies the cost based on corn and soybean values, but it could also consider other variables such as weather, competition among producers, producer bankruptcies, transportation costs, and market volume fluctuations. Note that by including more variables and interrelationships, the ability to determine potential impacts on McNuggets' profit becomes complex. The Monte Carlo method assigns random data to the various variables and correlates them with McDonald's profit, understanding a fixed price. Randomness will determine critical moments that anticipate the executive team's understanding of the random scenario and determine their actions. In negotiations, it is very useful because it defines "win-win" conditions, not based on the current agreement, but on the impact that a particular agreement can have on the business.

In the Monte Carlo method, the results of various actions are tested. Therefore, a negotiator can select a portion (sampling) of clients and suppliers and define specific approaches, evaluating counterarguments and outcomes. Modeling involves defining random variables such as business reduction, business increase, exchange rates, commodity prices, competition, commercial disinterest, and any creative approach that requires a response.

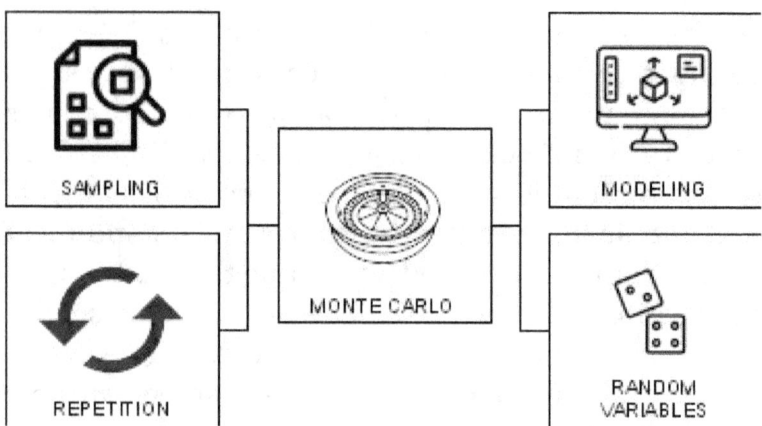

The repetition of approaches and variables, as well as customer responses, will determine patterns. It's important to work with logical variables that prevent random variables from devaluing the negotiation.

Vanguard Group is the world's largest investment manager, managing over 7 trillion dollars. Vanguard was founded in 1974 by Jack Bogle and emphasizes a philosophy of simplicity, diversification, and patience. For Jack, investors should avoid the euphoria of identifying momentum and focus on the strategy and negotiations of assets in a diversified and long-term model. In 2008, Vanguard was closely evaluated because investors wanted to know if the diversification approach was sustainable under extreme conditions. The Vanguard 500 fund presents consistent gains and, despite taking advantage of momentum waves, has an impressive average performance, providing security to shareholders. Trading an asset (stocks) is similar to commercial negotiations when choosing customers or suppliers through an agreement; the configuration of the company's portfolio is defined. The management of commercial agreements in negotiations defines the company's performance, both in revenue generation and in cost control that determines profitability. A negotiator needs to consider their portfolio of customers or suppliers, not focusing on momentum but on consistency. For this, portfolio management is strategic and the basis for successful commercial negotiations.

The "mean-variance model" was developed by Harry Markowitz and earned him the Nobel Prize. In 1952, Markowitz presented something that serves as the basis for various investment funds, such as Vanguard. In this model, it is possible to determine configurations that define the balance between expected return and risk. Risk is determined by the volatility of asset prices, which, when diversified with other assets, result in stability. For Markowitz, it is a prerequisite for negotiators to be rational, and the risk statistics and the redefinition of the expected result are correlated. A negotiator can depend on an asset, customer, or supplier, so all performance is subject to a single variable. When the negotiator establishes a portfolio, multiplying assets, revenue, and costs, there is automatically a minimization of volatility, but also of expectations for results. Through the Markowitz model, the average historical return of a portfolio is determined, while at the same time, the variance and price fluctuations for the portfolio are evaluated. With a predefined portfolio, correlations are made, allowing an understanding of patterns and similarities in behaviors, which will prevent diversification in a portfolio with equated fluctuations. The portfolio is built rationally, understanding that the lower the risk, the lower the expected return. When building the portfolio supported by the Markowitz model, the negotiator defines how negotiations will be established.

The Markowitz model provides the negotiator with a broader view of the portfolio of clients and suppliers that require negotiation. It allows for the creation of an approach that diversifies options, although in some cases, it may require decisions that involve a trade-off, meaning that it's often necessary to forgo more advantageous offers or a long-term partnership to compose a portfolio with lower risk.

Markowitz's focus is on risk mitigation and often limits the possibilities of leveraged gains. The analysis associated with the model demonstrates that the portfolio can absorb emotional variations as well as managerial and financial failures on the part of clients and suppliers without compromising the business. The focus of the Markowitz model is strategic and defines the approach to negotiations.

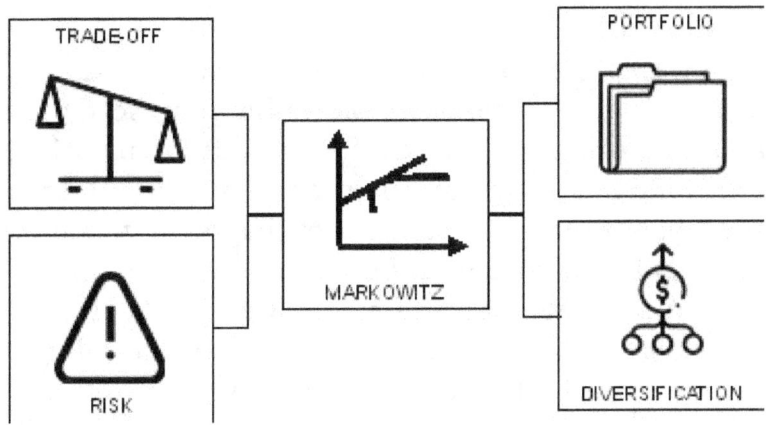

Skilled negotiators, in any aspect, ranging from critical negotiations like hostage situations to commercial negotiations for mergers and acquisitions, use statistics to anticipate potential scenarios, allowing the negotiator to prepare for pitfalls. Statistics define the probability of an event occurring; in this case, arguments and concessions can be evaluated without surprises. Any negotiation deals with the unexpected, from hidden claims to total inflexibility from the other party. Not knowing how to handle the unexpected brings emotional conditions to the negotiation table and can lead to unsuccessful and detrimental agreements for the corporation. A negotiator doesn't develop skills just to read body language or influence a single agreement, but to create value in every negotiation conducted. This determines the organization's risk, potential outcomes, and the configuration of assets, clients, and suppliers.

A negotiator will inevitably deal with the probability of an event occurring. Understanding probability and taking it into account when building scenarios and outcomes is crucial for proper preparation. Probability is a numerical measure that represents the chance of a specific event happening and is represented by a number from 0% to 100%. In games of chance, as well as in any situation, probability is calculable. In a dice game at a casino, the winner is determined when the sum of "seven" or "eleven" occurs; in this game, the probability of winning is 49.29%. In the game of roulette, however, the probability of hitting an exact number drops to 2.70%. The casino offers a higher reward to players who take risks with low probabilities, motivating players in exchange for a possible reward. Negotiators should not be tempted by the excitement of high gains but should have a stable portfolio that allows them to take controlled risks.

When Disney bought Pixar for $7.4 billion, there was a probability that the deal would be leveraged. The investment was insignificant and low-risk compared to the outcome. Disney diversified its products in the same segment and used "Toy Story" and "Monsters, Inc." to generate revenue, but also created successes like "Frozen," "UP," and "Zootopia" with the acquired animation technology. Steve Jobs, by anchoring the purchase price and accepting Disney shares, succeeded because he diversified his assets into Disney shares, which appreciated only due to the success of the animation market. There was a probability that the animation market would not grow exponentially, but the chances were low when combined with the successful films and Disney's cinematic reputation.

However, the merger of AOL and Time Warner for $164 billion showed a low probability of success. AOL's dial-up internet technology was outdated, which could be a problem in expanding the Time Warner brand. There was a risk of lack of synergy between the companies due to culture and industry segments. There was a risk of disagreements about strategic decisions regarding investment priorities and results management. AOL took high risks by investing substantial capital in the merger with Time Warner, despite its leadership position in the dial-up internet segment; there was no coherence in how the invested capital could return to AOL. Associating rationality with a business deal, such as the acquisition of Pixar or the merger with Time Warner, allows the construction of logical scenarios and the determination of the probability of success.

In negotiations, the agreement should be based on logical principles defined by rational premises and criteria that allow for measuring success. An agreement that suggests the possibility of a "win-lose" outcome should be evaluated from the perspective of probability and its impact on business. Taking high risks in pursuit of large rewards leads to frustration when the portfolio is not designed to absorb failures. The negotiator needs to assess dominance conditions, strategic balance to define arguments and concessions that recognize an agreement as part of a whole, not just an isolated event. The "positive bias" brings the perception that the agreement will have positive results, which is a fallacy when not supported by logic, statistics, and probability. A failed agreement can occur, but it should not be a surprise to the negotiator, as a negative scenario can always be drawn up, even with a low probability of occurring. Thus, the negotiator and the company prepare for likely negative conditions.

[Chapter 6] Game Theory

"Game theory provides a precise way to formulate the informal notion of strategy."

(John von Neumann)

In 1998, fishermen in Bonaire, a Caribbean island, faced a significant local problem in which they employed the "encircling fishing" technique. This technique involved surrounding entire schools of fish with nets and pulling them onto the beach. While this method was highly efficient, it resulted in a decrease in the quantity of fish in the region. Consequently, the government of Bonaire decided to implement conservation policies by prohibiting "encircling fishing" around the island. This directly affected the livelihoods of the fishermen and their families, leading to a standoff between the fishermen and the government.

As a solution, two options were offered to the fishermen: they could choose between "encircling fishing" or sustainable fishing using hooks and lines. However, even with these alternatives, it was crucial for the government of Bonaire to persuade the fishermen that sustainable fishing was the best long-term option. Cooperation among the fishermen was essential for the recovery of the fish population and the preservation of the marine habitat's quality.

The problem lay in the fact that merely showcasing the long-term benefits wouldn't guarantee the fishermen's adherence. If only a few of them opted for sustainable fishing, "encircling fishing" would continue to harm sustainable fishing, jeopardizing the fish's survival. The government of Bonaire adopted an intelligent and cooperation-focused approach. In addition to educating the fishermen about the risks to the marine habitat, they offered financial compensation, rewards for those who adopted sustainable fishing, as well as training and equipment. This approach sparked collective interest and resulted in mass participation.

Game theory is a mathematical specialty that studies the behavior of agents in situations of interdependence, where one agent's actions affect the outcomes of others involved. It complements logic and statistical approaches. John Von Neumann and Oskar Morgenstern developed this mathematical science with the aim of anticipating the strategic moves of players in economic, political, and wartime environments. Von Neumann observed that players made decisions considering the choices of others, making the prediction of individual and joint outcomes the correlation of decisions made by all players combined. In collaborative environments, players adjust their strategies to balance with the market. However, in conflict and competitive environments, players adapt their strategies to gauge and confront forces, aiming for a dominant position. For Von Neumann, the interrelationships were calculated mathematically, and statistical proportions defined likely scenarios.

In the field of negotiations, game theory enables the understanding of other players' strategies, the determination of probabilities, and the redesign of specific strategic approaches. By comprehending the counterpart's strategy, it is possible to establish positions, arguments, and concessions that result in either a cooperative or conflicting environment. In a game involving two or more players, it is possible to determine whether the players adopt strategies for a zero-sum game, where one player only wins if others lose, or a non-zero-sum game, in which the strategies of both oneself and others influence the outcomes of all involved, depending on the combinations of established strategies and dominant positions.

A "win-win" game does not imply that all players win, but rather that combined strategies lead to smaller losses and balance in the outcomes of the participants. When a first seller offers disproportionately high prices to the buyer, it encourages the buyer to adjust their purchasing strategy and seek a second seller, forcing the first seller to revise their strategy and lower prices to avoid losing revenue or customers. This dynamic is similar when a buyer pressures for unilateral reductions and compels the supplier to reposition itself. The dynamics of game theory utilize logic to compose moves and statistics to determine and measure the probability of repositioning. It is important to understand the barriers, incentives, and rewards that drive repositioning, which can be either rational or emotional.

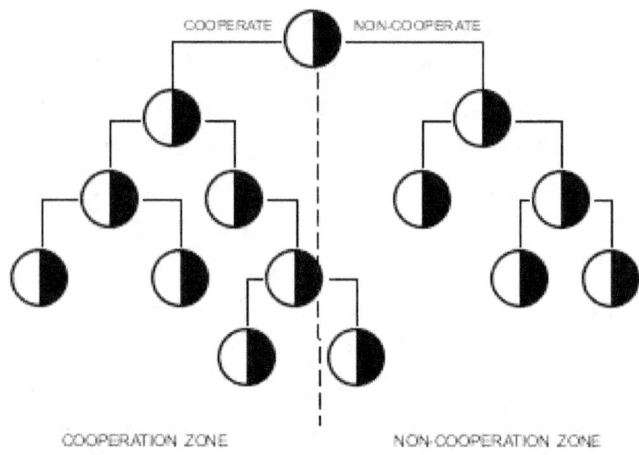

COOPERATION ZONE   NON-COOPERATION ZONE

In 2016, hackers known as "The Shadow Brokers" auctioned off stolen confidential information from the NSA. A public auction in bitcoins was opened, and if there were no bids, the information would be leaked. The hackers did not receive any bids, but they also did not leak the information. A second auction was initiated, this time with an initial value of ten thousand bitcoins, but it also did not succeed. The hackers' approach is in line with the science of game theory. The auction forced a zero-sum game, where only one player would have access to the information. However, the scenario of information leakage inhibited the players' actions, as they were afraid of making the highest bid and still having the information leaked. The auction is a game that determines a winner based on the simple rule of the highest bid, with only one player receiving the reward.

When using game theory to associate players' strategies and redesign one's own strategy, it is possible to identify defined moves aimed at cooperation or conflict. The emotional approach of "risk aversion" suggests unique opportunities, inciting a sense of urgency. However, when the same offer is perceived as a "bluff," players can counter the emotional approach. A buyer who requests a 20% discount from the seller, claiming that the business will move to the competition, places themselves in a dominant position and forces a conflicting action if there is no logical basis or if the supplier does not have significant room for a counteroffer. The buyer assumes a risk by forcing a zero-sum situation. Zero-sum approaches can destroy relationships, as they compel the counterpart to redesign their strategy in the face of imminent risk. Game theory ensures that business approaches can be structured in a way where logical and probable scenarios define arguments perceived as cooperative. "Bluffing" is only successful if the counterpart does not associate scenarios of cooperation and conflict. In this case, emotion drives flight or confrontation, characteristics that are determinants among negotiators without a rationalized plan.

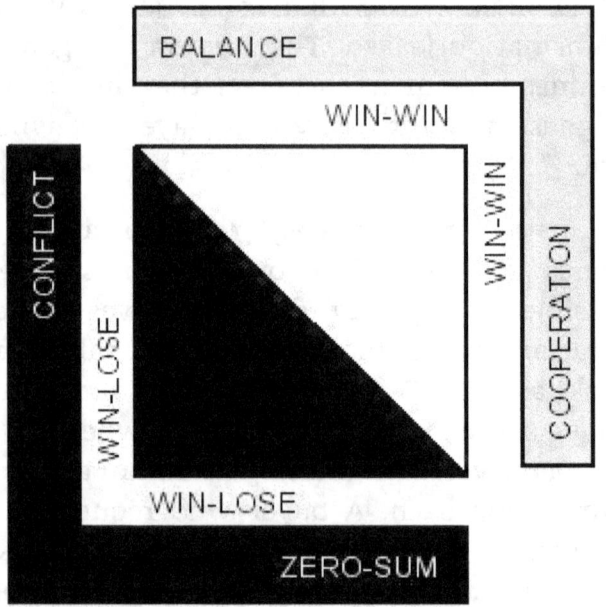

In 2008, Christopher Nolan released "The Dark Knight," a critical and commercial success. Heath Ledger portrayed the Joker, and Christian Bale portrayed Batman. In this film, an iconic scene depicts a game promoted by the Joker, where the players are civilians and prisoners on different boats. Each group of players receives a detonator capable of blowing up the opponent's boat. The rule established by the Joker imposes a zero-sum game, where to survive, one must blow up the opponent's boat; otherwise, both boats will explode at midnight. Nolan showcased a classic dynamic of game theory where the decision to cooperate or betray would determine the outcome. Despite the film raising moral questions and establishing a less likely scenario where neither boat explodes, game theory would suggest blowing up the opponent's boat as quickly as possible, albeit under the significant risk of being blown up first. Experienced negotiators need to have clarity about potential scenarios and the most likely resolution, whether in a cooperative or conflict-oriented approach. In "The Dark Knight," it is possible to outline a "cooperative" scenario where no detonator is activated, resulting in a widespread explosion, another scenario of "mutual betrayal" where the detonators are activated simultaneously, and two scenarios of betrayal and cooperation where the one who cooperates is detonated. In game theory, the probability of betrayal is amplified when a time limit is introduced. Therefore, rationally, the boat scene in the Batman movie would have had a more dramatic outcome.

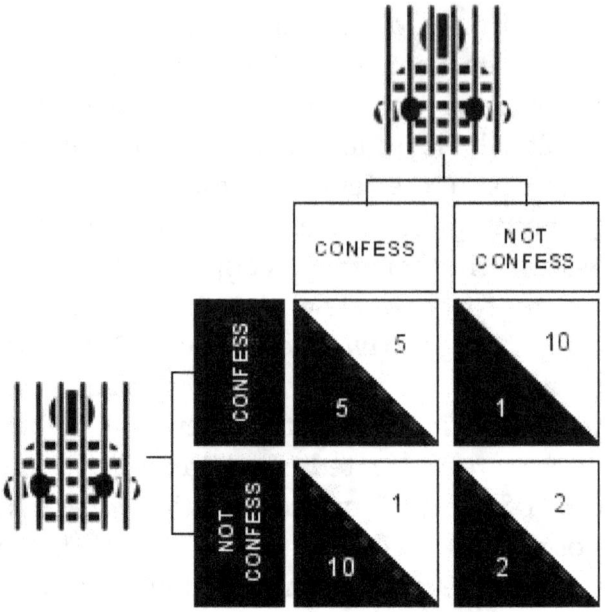

The modeling of a game with two players assigns interaction between cooperating and betraying at the expense of a likely outcome in pre-established scenarios. A classic game is the 'prisoner's dilemma,' in which two prisoners are interrogated individually, offered the option to 'confess' or 'not confess' to the crime. The penalty is assigned based on the correlation of responses. The first scenario occurs when both prisoners confess, resulting in a five-year prison sentence for both. Two other scenarios are defined when one decides to confess and the other does not: in this case, the one who confesses has their sentence reduced to one year, while the other prisoner receives ten years in prison. The last scenario occurs when neither of the prisoners confesses, resulting in a two-year prison sentence for each. In game theory, there is a graphical representation that allows for reflecting and associating results for each possible configuration. The iterations show how players can position themselves and the related consequences. This modeling allows for assigning probabilities based on logic, determining the most likely scenario and the best position to take.

In negotiations, the functionality of the graphical representation is developed as arguments, criteria, concessions, and positions are understood. Thus, it is possible to determine, in a game with two or more players, the approach of 'cooperation' and 'non-cooperation,' which allows for determining possible and likely results. Skilled negotiators intuitively use game theory and define strategies and approaches that underlie possible scenarios. For example, a seller may request a price increase for one customer while offering a reduction to another. Even so, they are cooperating since the strategy is adapted to the segment in which the customers operate and the risk balance in the portfolio. A 'win-win' negotiation is much more related to the balance of strategies among various players than to everyone having exactly the same profit margin. In game theory, a scenario called the 'Nash Equilibrium' is highlighted, determining the scenario in which players are encouraged to maintain their strategies, leading to specific player strategies in favor of mutual trade balance. This scenario shows that negotiators cannot focus solely on their isolated strategy but must understand the strategies of others and adapt their position to the detriment of the best individual benefit.

In 1990, American Airlines, Delta Air Lines, and United Airlines were accused of participating in a cartel to fix airfare prices and restrict competition. The accusations included coordination to increase fares and fees, limit seat availability on certain routes, and manipulate prices to the detriment of consumers. The dynamics of the 'prisoner's dilemma' were characterized in this situation, where companies cooperated to mutually increase airfare prices. Game theory also determines illegal moves, requiring more drastic actions when identified. In the case of airlines, by setting slightly higher prices without the possibility of healthy competition, despite coordinated cooperation, consumers were harmed. In this case, the dynamics are in a zero-sum game, where for the airlines to win, consumers had to lose, defining an illegal action. The dilemma was between 'increasing' and 'not increasing' prices. When companies realized that 'increasing' prices coordinately did not require efforts for productivity and value creation, they were automatically creating a cartel, where routes were adjusted to balance revenues and profits in a predetermined oligopoly.

Three approaches define how negotiators adapt strategies to maximize results in a setting associated with cooperation and conflict. These approaches seek to configure the type of game that players will engage in and look for players willing to submit to established rules. A strategic negotiating approach defines dominant positions and rules that underlie how players should position themselves to adapt to the designed environment. A strategic approach may not always accommodate players, so adjustments must be reconsidered for strategic alignment, making negotiations feasible.

The first approach is the "conflicting games" strategy. In this approach, rewards are coerced, promoting non-cooperation. The concept of zero-sum leads players to challenge each other for a winning position, being willing to accept rules that assign dominance, with a focus on "all or nothing." The approach of "conflicting games" is observed in auctions and the commodities market, where prices fluctuate according to supply and demand dynamics. In auctions, only the best offer leads to the reward, while in commodities, producers raise prices when there is high demand, and only those willing to pay a higher value receive the commodity since it is known that there is not enough for everyone. This creates a zero-sum approach in which commodity producers benefit from scarcity. Exclusive products can lead to a conflicting game when the supplier seeks to dominate the business relationship due to a lack of options for the buyer, raising prices without logical justification and putting the buyer in a hostage position. It is not only the seller who has the privilege of creating a conflicting game; the buyer, by creating a competitive environment and motivating sellers to offer prices in exchange for participation in the business, also develops an environment conducive to rivalry, where players challenge each other in a zero-sum outcome.

In the "conflicting games" approach, movements can be observed in the automotive sector, where purchasing power is immersed in conflict rules. New releases force suppliers to compete on prices to secure the deal. In addition to low costs, the rules need to align with specific criteria of quality, logistics, and legality. The conflicting approach reduces the number of players and puts vehicle manufacturers in a less privileged position. "Conflicting games" in the sector are not based solely on the purchasing power of large manufacturers but also on market dynamics. Car end consumers are attracted to new releases and seek the best cost-benefit since this decision will last for years. Sales infrastructure and the immediate availability of products influence competition. Therefore, companies like Volkswagen have a better chance of competing in "conflicting games" because they have easier access to the end customer and scale to influence the supply chain. Volkswagen, due to its size, had an advantage over Fiat and Peugeot until both companies merged into Stellantis. Fiat and Peugeot, upon realizing the "conflicting games," had to adapt their strategy to compete with companies like Volkswagen and Toyota. In the automotive sector, there is no strategic cooperation, and therefore specific segments, such as compact and utility vehicles, need to be adequately planned to allow investments to be recovered with an adequate profit margin. The creation of Stellantis in 2021 marks a significant change in cooperation among automotive companies to compete in a "conflicting game." Both Fiat and Peugeot have revised their strategies, which will change how they negotiate with consumers and suppliers.

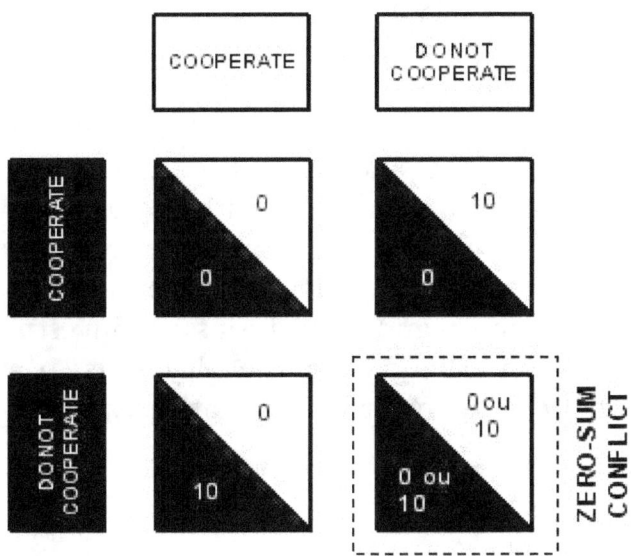

The second approach is the "cooperative games" strategy, in which strategies are developed taking into account the position of competitors. In "cooperative games," the value lies in avoiding large-scale conflicts, and the strategy is designed so that revenue is allocated to specific segments with little competition. In cooperation, players offer distinct options and adapt strategies, providing space for other players as long as there is no direct confrontation on a large scale. In "cooperative games," the figure of John Nash is recognized because he was able to prove that naturally, the market tends to balance, recognizing that dynamics and negotiation strategies are adapted over time to balance results. For John Nash, the "Nash Equilibrium" scenario determines that players will adjust their strategies when the result is influenced or when the strategies of other players affect the possibility of maximizing a balance in satisfactory results. "Cooperative games" suggest a balanced scenario that underlies significant changes in the strategies of players to maximize results without involving direct confrontation with competitors. The negotiation strategy can be based on the product portfolio, strategic partnerships, specific market segments, mergers and acquisitions, and investments in innovation. The goal of the players is to avoid conflict, directing toward a cooperative dynamic.

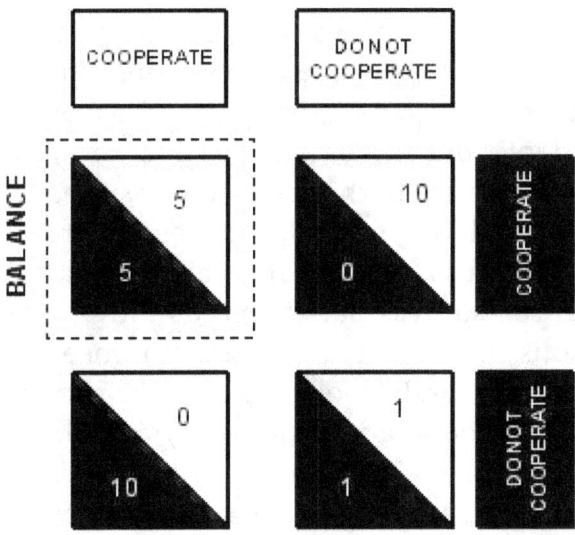

In the approach of "cooperative games," the pharmaceutical industry plays a significant role that positions companies in this specific configuration. Pharmaceutical companies allocate a portion of their revenue to the development of new products. The healthcare sector is vast and offers opportunities for various companies to operate in specific diseases and patient groups. This allows different solutions to be presented for the same disease, addressing specific patient needs. For example, in the diabetes segment, companies like Sanofi, Novo Nordisk, and Eli Lilly collaborate with academic institutions and startups to develop innovative products. This approach ensures that competing companies do not heavily invest in the same solution, minimizing direct competition and providing global protection through intellectual property.

Two competing companies can cooperate in the development of the same diabetes solution but with a focus on different aspects, such as duration or method of administration. For instance, Humalog and NovoLog are both fast-acting insulins, but they have adjusted their formulas to meet different patient needs. Similarly, long-acting insulins like Basaglar and Lantus address patient needs differently. These variations in formulation aim to meet different requirements and involve specific investments and approvals. Cooperation not only avoids conflicts over the same market but also offers more options to patients. Opting for cooperation in the pharmaceutical industry results in investments focused on specific, patented solutions that yield consistent results over the years.

The third approach is the strategy of "adaptive games," which involves constant adjustments in strategies during repetitive negotiations, considering the counterpart's positioning and market changes. Companies are constantly reinventing themselves, and despite trends for cooperation or conflict, as seen in the automotive and pharmaceutical industries, adaptation is often necessary due to the market's acceptance of certain strategies.

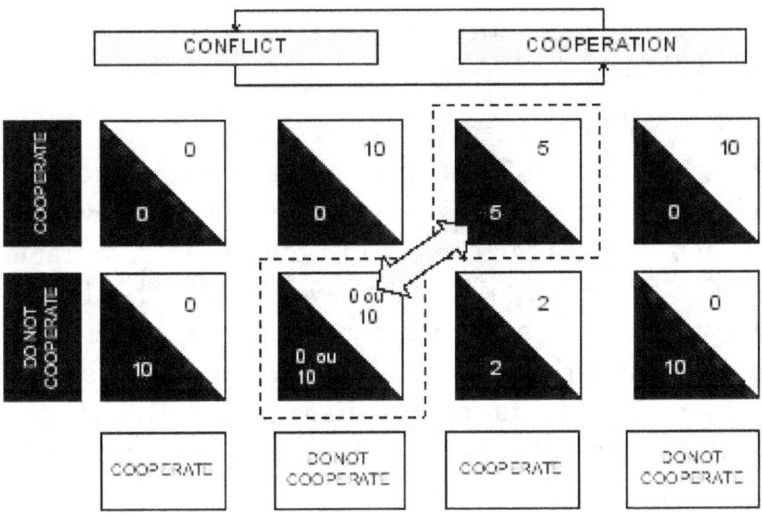

For example, Tesla adapted its strategy to avoid direct competition with combustion-engine vehicles, and its success in this approach attracted major automakers. Netflix also had to adapt its strategy by eliminating the local video rental market and facing new heavyweight competitors like HBO, Amazon, and Apple. When a company triggers significant market changes, an "adaptive game" is expected from competitors, sellers, and buyers.

"Adaptive games" result in a chaotic business environment filled with opportunities and threats for those who can adapt quickly and understand the new rules of the game. This approach takes into account the players' positions in both the previous and current configurations, seeking to understand how the quadrants are being redefined. Through game theory, it is possible to understand and predict likely moves by negotiators with cooperative or conflicting tendencies.

For example, in the past, household appliances were designed to last, with high prices, and consumers viewed them as long-term investments. However, Chinese manufacturers introduced less durable products with significantly lower prices. This forced Western companies to adapt, resulting in increased price competitiveness. The nylon market is also undergoing adaptation due to raw material shortages and the need to develop alternatives to maintain automotive production.

Companies like BASF, DuPont, Celanese, DSM, and Lanxess, as well as the entire automotive industry, have had to adapt to a new approach to nylon. The nylon market involves global companies with operations in various countries and thousands of customers, each with specific formulation needs. Before the shortage, the approach was cooperative, with components designed for specific nylons that remained as a unique raw material. However, the lack of nylon led to production stoppages and losses, forcing the development of alternative nylon options.

This adaptation led customers to develop components with alternative options to minimize supply risks in case one of the sources was unavailable. This also introduced price competitiveness, which was not common in a cooperative market. The nylon market is adapting to a condition that could turn nylon into a commodity, potentially reshaping the market's configuration.

BASF, as a major nylon producer, will need to adapt to a market where Celanese acquired DuPont and Lanxess purchased DSM. Additionally, the transition to electric vehicles and government investments is accelerating the development of new products that require nylon as a raw material. Negotiations should continue in a "conflict game" but with a cooperative inclination, with competitive pricing approaches, supply guarantees, strategic development partnerships, and exclusive contracts for differentiated benefits. Customers will benefit from more options and a nylon market seeking to reintroduce a cooperative environment. Customers, recognizing limited options, will seek to balance negotiations for prices that benefit their return on investment. "Adaptive games" require efforts from both sides, customers and suppliers, in pursuit of balance, and this should result in more acquisitions, mergers, and partnerships among producers, reducing the need for multiple approvals by customers in favor of return on investment. Negotiators will take advantage of adaptive moments to offer lower prices and better profit margins, which are expected to be more accepted by producers in the short term.

[Part 3] The Art of Agreement

"The secret of achievement is knowing when to stop."

Albert Einstein

Negotiating, arguing, and compromising are fundamental actions in a negotiation that enable reaching an agreement. However, what's important is reaching a conclusion, whether it's an agreement or not. The process of closing a deal and concluding a negotiation can involve emotional aspects that influence procrastination or generate anxiety. The more rationality, variables, analysis, and people are involved in a negotiation process, the more complex the conclusion process can be. The concept of "win-win" sometimes makes conclusions difficult because it's emotionally easier to accept a closed negotiation when it's clear that someone came out at a disadvantage in the process.

In 1998, Northern Ireland signed the Belfast Agreement, a peace agreement that was achieved through patience and diplomacy. Conflicts in the region began three decades before the agreement's signing and involved religious issues, civil rights, nationalism, and ideology—complex criteria and variables that divided the country. The religious communities were divided between Catholics and Protestants, which was the main cause of the conflict, as Catholics sought the unification of Ireland while Protestants wished to remain part of the United Kingdom.

In 1969, the UK, seeking a quick solution, sent the army to contain the violence and resolve the disputes. However, what was meant to be a temporary measure became long-lasting and intensified the activities of paramilitary groups, such as the Catholic-oriented IRA (Irish Republican Army) and the Protestant-oriented UVF (Ulster Volunteer Force). These radical paramilitary groups carried out bombings, armed conflicts, and assassinations, exposing the conflict in Northern Ireland to the world and putting pressure on the British and Irish governments.

Negotiations with the IRA and UVF needed to be mediated by the UK and Ireland, which had to cooperate to reach a conclusion. However, all the emotional pressure and historical military events made the IRA and UVF cautious. Tony Blair and Bertie Ahern played significant roles in the negotiations, demonstrating cooperation and patience to reach an agreement. To do so, they had to personally engage in negotiations with the IRA and UVF. Both politicians were successful in their approaches, resulting in the Belfast Agreement, based on power-sharing and the pursuit of peace, thus formalizing the end of a decades-long conflict.

An agreement represents the conclusion of a negotiation process that can last hours or years. General criteria are often evident and easy to identify, and the negotiators' approach plays a crucial role in resolution. Impatient negotiators can force situations that escalate conflicts, distorting criteria and creating new variables. Negotiators' skill lies in seeking balanced and criteria-appropriate solutions in a given conflict, with a sole focus on achieving a coherent agreement.

[Chapter 7] Procrastination and Cognition

"You cannot escape tomorrow's responsibilities by avoiding them today."

(Abraham Lincoln)

In 1948, Charles Lazarus opened a baby products store in Washington DC. Lazarus was a brilliant entrepreneur who transformed this baby products store into the largest toy chain in the USA, reaching its peak revenue in the 1980s, with $12 billion per year. Toy "R" Us had a successful business model where customers could interact with toys, and the brand established megastores across the USA with creative advertising and an enviable selection of toys. Toy "R" Us experienced peak sales during the Christmas season.

However, with the advent of the internet, Lazarus didn't believe that people would trade the physical interaction with toys for the convenience of a click. Amazon was founded in the same year Lazarus retired in 1994, and the internet was still an unknown gamble. However, e-commerce grew rapidly, and Amazon, after investing in online book sales, shifted its focus to toys. Toy "R" Us saw a decline in revenue, acknowledging the influence of the internet but not to the extent of redirecting investments toward developing e-commerce instead of opening new stores. Investment decisions were delayed for 7 years until the company launched a website. However, this site did not offer a solid logistical framework, which damaged the company's reputation. With reduced demand and assets and stagnant inventory in stores, Toy "R" Us suffered severe cash flow impacts, forcing it into debt and preventing investments in innovation and new products, opening the door for Amazon, eBay, Walmart, Target, and their digital stores. In 2017, the company filed for bankruptcy.

Advancing decisions should not be confused with patience. There is an emotional bias that needs to be understood with rationality and logic, avoiding procrastination, which can result in preemptive action before it's too late. Negotiators rely on a balance between emotional and rational sense to manage an agreement. Procrastination, the act of delaying decisions in pursuit of a perfect agreement, is often motivated by the "win-lose" mentality.

Psychology treats procrastination as a lack of motivation, conditioned behavior, emotional trauma, dysfunctional cognitive patterns, social influence, and self-regulation capability. Learning negotiation techniques and creating closure scenarios is irrelevant if a negotiator doesn't develop the ability to conclude. Identifying procrastination is difficult because it's not just related to decision delays but also to the postponement of necessary tasks for closure. The procrastinating negotiator often seeks continued concessions from the counterpart, as their focus is on filling emotional gaps. The act of procrastination can be emotionally manipulated, forcing "win-lose" scenarios and dealing with options that relieve emotional pressure and satisfy the procrastinator.

Procrastination is chronic and harms the results and reputation of the negotiator and the company they represent. It's important to identify actions or lack thereof indicating that a particular negotiation is being procrastinated. Simple techniques like noting the next steps and completion dates facilitate identifying delays. Delay is not always evidence of procrastination and needs to be evaluated based on the source of the delay or which side of the negotiating table is demanding more deadline extensions. When confirming procrastination as a behavioral pattern, it's essential to understand the emotional cause or bureaucratic process behind it. Procrastination can be individual or cultural, reflecting a seller's reluctance to confirm a price reduction or a buyer's resistance to accepting a price increase, even if the arguments are legitimate.

Agreements need to follow a process with a beginning, middle, and end. Therefore, it's important to document conclusion premises, negotiation progress, and closing recommendations to assist the decision-making process. The more people involved in the decision, the more likely delays will occur, a characteristic of vertical companies that limit autonomy and promote internal bureaucracy to postpone decisions. In negotiations, one should not expect to have access to all the variables and information needed to decide. It's important to use logic, probability, and game theory to complement scenarios and evaluate consequences. Organizational cultures based on procrastination are detrimental to a company's results. Therefore, it's crucial to implement procedures that rationally underpin decisions, share responsibilities, and promote rational agreements. A procedure can be developed in four steps: the first is recognizing deadlines and changes, where a simple date and progress recording system can be a solution. The second step involves highlighting progress since complex negotiations may justify delays, but progress is of great importance. The third step is defining a technology that ensures proper documentation and involves parties in sharing responsibilities because the more concessions, consequences, claims, arguments, and criteria are shared, the more assertive the agreement. The last step is to keep a record of people and authorities who procrastinate decisions or refuse agreements, enabling the tracking of participants, collaborators, and blockers of an agreement.

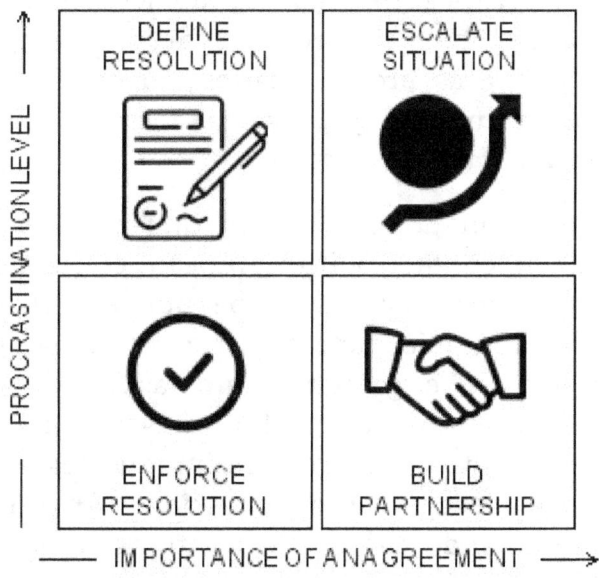

In 1962, the USA confirmed the installation of Soviet missiles in Cuba, which alerted to a direct threat to American hegemony and its population. This occurred during the Cold War, generating widespread panic and pressuring American President

John F. Kennedy to adopt a diplomatic approach to resolve the situation with the Soviet Union. However, the public perceived Kennedy's response as procrastination and demanded immediate retaliation against Cuba. For two weeks, there were military movements in Cuban soil with no immediate action from the American government, increasing distress and popular pressure, along with the imminent threat of a nuclear conflict. President Kennedy chose to postpone any US military intervention and focused on diplomatic negotiations with Soviet leader Nikita Khrushchev. These negotiations, despite being seen by the public as procrastination, made significant progress, culminating in an agreement for the withdrawal of the missiles.

Procrastination doesn't always indicate weakness, especially in conflicts with significant consequences, where a patient approach can be more effective than impulsive and quick actions. Negotiations aimed at an agreement offer greater stability as they don't rely on force as a means of resolution. Negotiators who opt for force introduce emotions into the negotiation, which can lead to drastic actions followed by frustration and anger. Negotiations that avoid emotional reactions favor the construction of lasting agreements based on rational criteria and solutions. It's important to distinguish between procrastination and patience, with the latter highly recommended when waiting for the right moment for an agreement. Putting negotiators under pressure limits clarity and can lead to actions that trigger emotional reactions and retaliation.

There are signs that indicate procrastination, such as avoiding meetings, constant delays in counter-proposals, superficiality in discussing the criteria to be negotiated, agreements subject to constant revisions, and the introduction of new criteria. The body language of a procrastinator often conveys uncertainty, with hesitation in defining positions and evasive eye contact. The procrastinator often seeks social confirmation and has difficulty committing to an agreement. In negotiations with procrastinators, it's important to be objective and sometimes break the negotiation into smaller, emotionally manageable parts. Patience is a valuable ally when dealing with unstable negotiators who seek to argue and avoid confrontation to relieve emotional pressure. In negotiations where uncertainty is a factor, it's essential to review and formalize progress, providing cognitive reassurance and preventing emotional imbalances. A patient approach, with open-ended questions guiding thought and defining key criteria for an agreement, is important in communications that demonstrate attention and commitment.

A negotiator's strategy is not always obvious to external observers and can sometimes be situational. The negotiation strategy can be planned to create chaos and emotional confusion, making the agreement more direct, as reason and emotion converge towards a specific outcome. In this case, the perception of procrastination is an influencing element. In April 2022, Elon Musk acquired 9% of Twitter's shares, becoming the largest individual shareholder in the company. However, Musk had a strategy that was only revealed after the purchase was completed. He planned to take Twitter private and rename it "X." The first step was to make a public offer for the company and formalize it, offering a price that was 38% above the stock's value. Among the established criteria, there was a specific one that required Twitter to disclose the total number of users and the percentage of fake accounts. Shareholders' pressure on the board created internal turmoil within the company, leading to the dismissal of top executives, a halt in hiring, company restructuring, and difficulties in confirming the percentage of fake accounts. Externally, it was not clear whether Twitter's board and major shareholders were buying time or procrastinating a decision. Musk withdrew his purchase offer, citing a lack of transparency on the requested criteria. The fake account issue didn't have a well-grounded technical solution, exposing Twitter's technical team. However, since Musk had formalized the offer, there was a legal obligation, and new deadlines were set, putting more pressure on programmers and top management. Twitter's shareholders and board eventually agreed to sell to Musk for $44 billion, but they still couldn't provide an accurate percentage of fake accounts, violating a criterion that led Elon Musk to withdraw the purchase. This resulted in a legal proceeding in court, which ruled in favor of Twitter, forcing Musk to accept the purchase or face market manipulation charges. Six months after the initial offer, Musk officially acquired Twitter.

The Twitter acquisition demonstrated significant emotional pressure on both sides of the negotiation table, with loss aversion triggers causing frustration. This moved beyond the realm of reason when taken to court. Media pressure exposed both Twitter's board and Elon Musk regarding the purchase. While there was an offer on the table that wasn't contested, the fake accounts criterion became the main obstacle to the agreement, creating an external perception of procrastination by both parties. The technical criterion for determining the percentage of fake accounts was complex and subject to different calculation methodologies, which facilitated disagreements. However, the other party didn't present a solution.

In procrastinating processes, it's common to use cognitive stress to confuse the other party, gain time, or cancel a negotiation that was previously poorly positioned. Cognitive stress results from situations of stress, fatigue, and exposure, leading people to process information partially and make decisions without complete analysis. Psychological factors suggest that negotiators avoid rational decisions when cognitive pressure makes the process more complex than simply following authority expectations. In the case of Twitter, the $44 billion offer was easy to process, but determining the percentage of fake accounts was not. This eventually led to a situation where a third party had to intervene to make a decision, as complex cognitive processing was expected, and as a result, the decision would likely favor Twitter.

In cognitive psychology, three cognitive biases enable negotiators to steer their negotiations by adapting their approach to human cognitive limitations. The "confirmation bias" is the first of these cognitive limitations, leading the negotiator to accept arguments and offers based on their pre-existing beliefs. The "availability bias" is the second cognitive limitation, causing the negotiator to simplify the agreement based on readily available information. The "loss aversion bias" is the third cognitive limitation and influences the negotiator to overlook negative information to avoid risks. A well-applied cognitive approach can mitigate procrastination, while its misuse can manipulate less experienced negotiators.

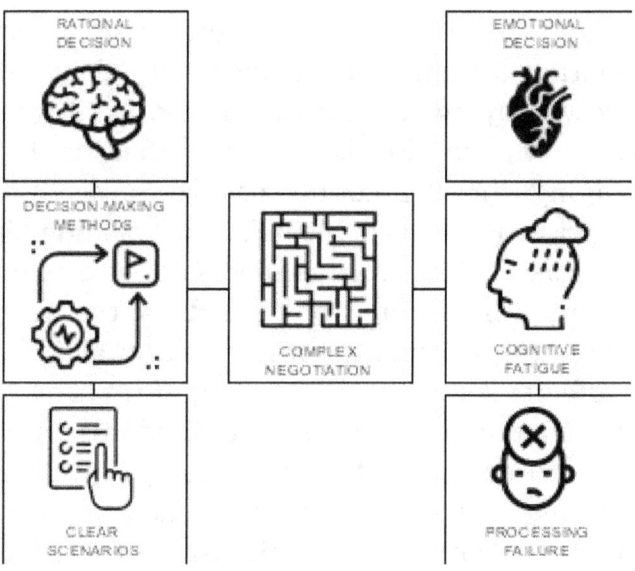

Through the "confirmation bias," negotiators filter information with the aim of gaining advantages and safeguarding their own interests. This approach aims for a "win-lose" outcome, concealing relevant information and exploiting the cognitive limitation of the counterpart, who may not fully grasp the business or be unaware of relevant facts. In an attempt to influence the counterpart's decision, the negotiator chooses not to disclose weaknesses, such as product quality, initial offer conditions, and the precarious financial situation of the company. By selecting and concealing information, the negotiator steers the counterpart toward a conclusion that confirms only the positive aspects, especially when the commercial offer is advantageous. In this confirmation approach, when the "confirmation bias" is perceived in the counterpart, positive information is highlighted, exaggerating the positives and downplaying concerns. In the confirmation approach, information is also simplified, making it challenging for the counterpart to process. This allows prioritizing available information and using it as the basis for logically justified sales and purchase arguments. For example, one could use the inflation rate to request a total increase, even though inflation only affects some costs. The "confirmation bias" ensures that less experienced individuals overlook relevant criteria out of fear of losing, resulting in emotionally satisfying decisions, such as claiming it's the last opportunity, and the counterpart accepts without further arguments. When an agreement is closed based on the "confirmation bias," there is a high probability of new criteria and variables emerging later in the negotiation. Experienced buyers are critical thinkers who apply logic, statistics, and game theory, making it harder to manipulate them through the "confirmation bias."

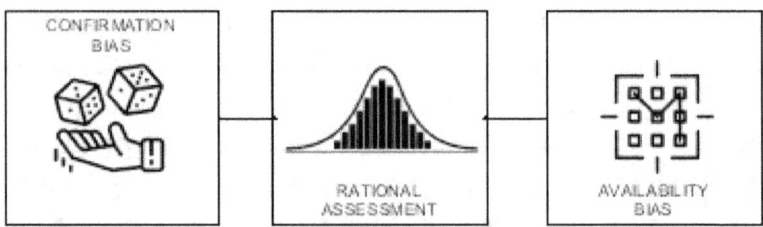

Inevitably, these cognitive biases intertwine, allowing negotiators to create creative options based on an understanding of the counterpart's behavior.

Through the "availability bias," it is possible to focus on and present only the conditions that favor the agreement. By introducing many variables into the negotiation, the counterpart may experience cognitive conflict, making decision-making difficult and leading to procrastination. In the availability approach, it is common to present packages or decision options, ensuring that the counterpart pays attention and arrives at their conclusions based on what has been presented. This enables manipulation or influence of the counterpart toward a specific decision, even if they believe they have the power of choice. For example, in cinemas, consumers are presented with sizes of small, medium, and large popcorn. Through the "availability bias," cinemas can influence consumers' decisions by simply adjusting the price of medium popcorn. If small popcorn costs $5 for 300 ml and large popcorn costs $10 for 900 ml, cinemas can induce consumers to consider a medium popcorn of 450 ml for $9 as an advantageous option, leading them to overlook the small popcorn. The "availability bias" presents few options, simplifying decision-making and allowing manipulation of unprepared negotiators in the desired direction. Experienced buyers create options based on the positions presented or bring their own options to the negotiation, ensuring a fairer and more organized negotiation.

When confronted with the confirmation and availability biases, there is no emotional trigger, only cognitive attenuation that inhibits processing and decision association. However, through the "loss aversion bias," cognitive processes collapse with emotion, forcing positions or prolonging procrastination. When negotiators adopt an approach involving emotions, less experienced counterparts naturally seek to escape or confront, inconsistent instincts that hinder a rational agreement. In negotiations involving cognitive processing, the introduction of the "loss aversion bias" focuses on the negative consequences of not closing the deal, creating a mental trigger that generates interest in closing the deal to avoid potential disadvantages. In this bias, the negotiator highlights possible losses and ensures that the counterpart views the offer as a unique opportunity, reinforcing that there will be no other chance. Furthermore, the emotional loss aversion approach suggests that if the deal is later considered bad, it will still be possible to backtrack and revise the agreed conditions. However, the counterpart is not expected to backtrack and reject the offer, as there is no intention of reimbursement. Sectors such as finance and real estate make use of loss aversion, presenting irresistible opportunities and guarantees but resorting to bureaucratic processes and procedures to reverse what was offered, resulting in less advantageous agreements. The "loss aversion bias" manipulates emotions by offering emergency options and non-existent guarantees. Experienced buyers understand the market and know that missed opportunities are rare, evaluating them based on statistical and logical analysis rather than succumbing to the seller's arguments. Loss aversion can be reversed by demonstrating to the buyer or seller that the current approach jeopardizes the relationship and will result in greater losses for the party making the offer. Approaches based on loss aversion should be eliminated from the outset.

It is important to understand the context of a negotiation, where players, criteria, and interests are recognized. In negotiations considered procrastinatory, expectations vary depending on the negotiator's approach. In the "win-win" scenario, the assumption that people understand when they are losing or winning is challenged, as most players tend to adopt a zero-sum game mentality. This makes it easier to recognize an advantageous outcome. On the other hand, the procrastinatory approach constantly changes agreements and criteria for its benefit and does not accept arguments that do not lead to a "win-lose" scenario. By adopting rational approaches, the negotiator avoids emotional and cognitive pitfalls and is able to identify when the counterpart is manipulating scenarios.

[Chapter 8] Focus and Consequence

"It's not enough to have made plans. We must execute them."

(Winston Churchill)

In September 1992, England was forced to withdraw the pound sterling from the European Exchange Rate Mechanism (ERM), which resulted in the elimination of the fixed exchange rate and the floating of the British currency. The British economy was already showing signs of weakening and facing economic challenges due to efforts to control inflation. Instability in the UK led to speculation in the financial markets and encouraged trading in currency assets in the futures market.

Short selling and buying is an investment strategy in which the trader bets on the decline or increase in the price of an asset by conducting a future sale operation. This approach requires information processing that demands emotional calm and analytical ability to choose the right time to act against the market. On September 16, 1992, the famous "Black Wednesday" occurred, which marked the history of the United Kingdom and propelled George Soros onto the world stage. Soros, along with other traders, bet against the pound sterling, but George Soros, at the age of 62 at the time, went further. He was convinced that the moment of the pound's devaluation had arrived and leveraged his short selling operations through the Quantum Fund, an action that made his team nervous due to the risks involved. After Black Wednesday, Soros closed out his short-selling operations, pocketing $1 billion in a single day. Those close to Soros report that this strategy was high-risk and created great pressure, but he returned home that night as if it were an ordinary day, such was his conviction that the UK would announce the currency's floatation. Soros's composure was crucial to the success of the Quantum Fund, his discipline in data analysis, and his rational approach to high-risk trading had always been characteristics of his style. The crisis of the British pound was just a large-scale event that he knew how to take advantage of.

Professional negotiators can develop special analysis patterns and have specific approaches for each negotiation situation. The emotional and rational models presented in this book serve as the basis for the construction of sophisticated and creative negotiations led by negotiators who can maintain minimal emotional involvement and assess the probability and logical consistency of a specific event. A negotiator's decision-making follows their own analyses and not a step-by-step script. Therefore, concepts such as MAPAN, game theory, Boolean logic, and Monte Carlo, as well as other rational tools, add knowledge, but it's the way a negotiator applies their skills that determines an extraordinary outcome.

Recognizing the possibility of a "win-win" is irrelevant when both parties at the negotiation table are seeking fair outcomes. In negotiations involving kidnappings, the police's focus is on ensuring the release of hostages with their lives, with the arrest of the kidnappers being a secondary priority. In this context, it can be said that the negotiation resulted in a "win-win." However, it's important to note that moral values and the recurrence of similar events can lead to a reevaluation of whether a kidnapping should result in a "win-win." Emotion can lead to a desire for the hostages to come out alive and the kidnappers to be arrested, resulting in a conflict between emotion and rationality and eventually leading to a "win-lose" scenario that distorts focus and complicates the outcome.

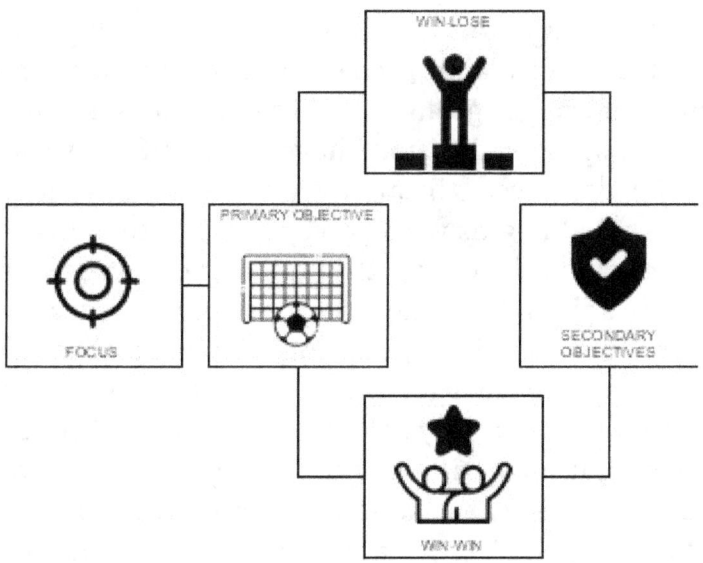

A negotiation should be designed to serve the interests of the company being represented or individual interests, as long as it does not involve the manipulation of information or irresponsibility. The pursuit of a "win-win" is not necessarily related to seeking an outcome in which everyone leaves the negotiation table satisfied. Instead, it's about creating a coherent strategy that establishes a balance, avoiding possible retaliations for future losses. Professional negotiators are fair and responsible in their planning, analysis, and approaches. They are also reasonable in their concessions and flexibility, but they know how to organize their strategies effectively and deal with losses.

Making a decision is a process of choosing one option among several available alternatives, based on the evaluation of information and objectives. The decision-making process involves cognitive and emotional stages grounded in the pursuit of survival. In neuroscience, decisions have a scientific basis and can be enhanced through training. It is a neural process that begins with perception and information gathering, followed by the association of relevant factors adapted to the environment and context. Senses such as vision, hearing, and touch are used to assess and recognize the best decision among available options. Physiologically, the neural process processes information, dividing it into intuitive (fast) and cognitive (slow) streams. The prefrontal cortex must be trained to create neural connections that minimize cognitive wear and tear and prepare the individual for adaptive situations. A well-developed and trained neural process allows for making more and better choices.

Effective negotiation should focus on the main goal. To do this, the negotiator needs to reflect on what is important to be agreed upon and what is secondary. A negotiation can focus on price, but it can also involve deadlines and additional services. When multiple variables are considered in the decision, the negotiator needs to create scenarios that allow for consolidation of understanding and comparisons. Financial indicators such as Net Present Value (NPV), Internal Rate of Return (IRR), and Payback Period (PAYBACK) help in this consolidation process.

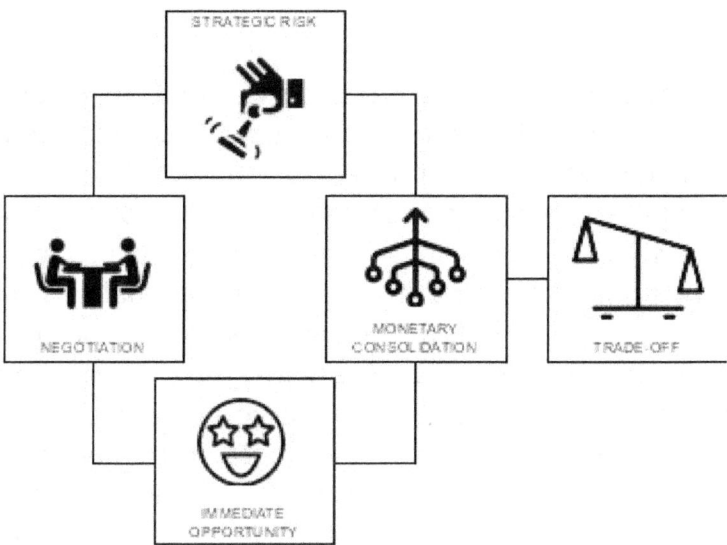

A negotiation involves emotional aspects, especially when there's a trade-off. A trade-off refers to decisions where a gain is accompanied by a loss, and since loss aversion often causes people to hesitate, it's important to have financial equations that evaluate the proposal as a whole. In vertical companies, the result of a negotiation is evaluated by authorities who usually don't have access to the entire process and tend to assess the outcome emotionally. Dealing with the emotional perceptions of authorities who don't accept the result due to insecurity should be minimized through transparency about the losses and gains, as well as reversal options, providing greater peace of mind to the decision-maker. By associating numbers with the advantages and disadvantages of the negotiation outcome, the negotiator is transforming emotional scenarios into rational ones.

More complex negotiations involve public opinion, and therefore, the result tends not to be accepted the same way by everyone, as emotional aspects can lead to negative perceptions of the negotiation's outcome. The negotiator must define the focus from the beginning, making it clear what the goal of the negotiation is. This minimizes misunderstandings of public opinion and increases the chances of acceptance given the established context. Influence plays a relevant role in the negotiation context, and it's necessary to educate opinion leaders and adjust the focus based on recommendations and expectations. In vertical companies where directors have distinct expectations, it's important to make the goal and focus transparent, ensuring that the main expectation is aligned.

In 2010, JC Penney reported negative margins for the first time since its founding in 1902. The company needed to reinvent itself, especially due to the growth of e-commerce and the success of Amazon. Shareholders sought a CEO with experience in technology and retail, anticipating that this would be the best choice for the new market scenario. By the end of 2011, a former executive from Target and Apple, with a successful track record, was invited to take on the role. However, JC Penney's case was unique and delicate, as there was pressure from shareholders due to recurring losses, a technological gap compared to competitors, a culture forged over more than 100 years, and a successful business model. The proposal from the former Apple executive focused not only on technology but on structural changes that would affect JC Penney's culture, customers, and partners, which raised concerns and led to the immediate dismissal of the board, which was replaced. In early 2012, a transformation plan was presented that generated positive emotional excitement in the market, immediately leading to an increase in the company's stock. JC Penney met shareholders' emotional expectations, but it needed to prove that the plan would deliver results. However, the decision-making process and execution harmed the company's results, being described by the market as "one of the most unsuccessful mandates in retail history." Ron Johnson approached JC Penney's business as if it were a startup, improperly allocated resources, and devalued loyal and core customers. Additionally, he manipulated suppliers and employees with promises that the company's cash flow would not allow.

As CEO, Ron rejected JC Penney's business model and chose to allocate resources to restructuring stores and creating a "fair" pricing policy, eliminating discounts and coupons and raising prices. The immediate reaction from customers was frustration and disinterest, resulting in revenue loss and the destruction of JC Penney's reputation, driving away potential customers. JC Penney was known for offering high-quality luxury items at affordable prices, but Ron decided to transform the company into a luxury retailer with inaccessible prices. JC Penney's communication advocated the "fair" pricing strategy, completely ignoring discount coupons. Ron eliminated an essential feature of the company for its customers, which was the excitement of finding discounts on luxury items, leading to the loss of the entire existing customer base. Throughout 2012, sales plummeted dramatically and continuously, with a -32% drop compared to 2011, marking the worst quarter in retail history. After about a year, Ron was removed from his position, but not all decisions could be easily reversed, causing serious consequences for JC Penney, including a cash flow collapse and the alienation of old and loyal customers who lost confidence in the company. Employees and suppliers also no longer saw JC Penney as a promising company, resulting in significant standoffs regarding efficiency and concessions, forcing the company to seek capital from banks. This triggered a spiral of debt that led JC Penney to file for bankruptcy in 2020.

Negotiators need to consider the consequences of their actions and proceed in a way that people understand the next steps. Forcing or manipulating actions without understanding the possible consequences in case of unfavorable outcomes negatively exposes the established plan. Presenting the focus and the expected outcome creates positive expectations, but when the focus is not met, it can generate frustration and put the negotiator in the spotlight. It's important to consider four key aspects that a negotiation with negative results can bring. The first aspect is organizational culture, where possible impacts on people's behaviors, which depend on the negotiation's outcome, are recognized. When negative consequences can significantly affect the culture, it's important to reconsider the focus. The second aspect is reputation with customers, assessing possible damage and how it can affect the perception of the company, impacting the willingness to do business with it. The third aspect is reputation with suppliers, considering how they view the company after an unsuccessful negotiation and how it can affect the business relationship. The fourth aspect is financial, evaluating the financial impact of an unsuccessful negotiation, including the possibility of the company going bankrupt in case of an extremely negative outcome. In case of a real threat to any of these factors, it's important to carefully review the negotiation, reassessing the emotional and rational aspects to determine the best approach or approaches to achieve the established focus.

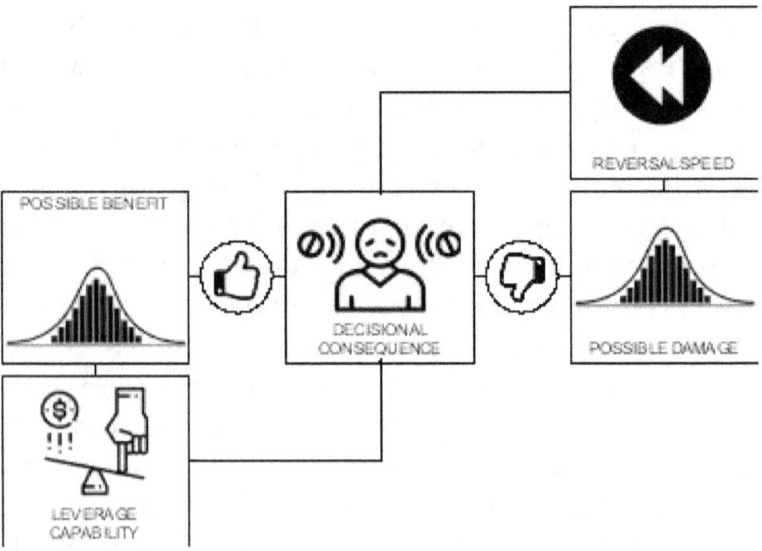

A well-defined negotiation with an established focus sets the process of approach and execution, anticipating benefits and damages, understanding a margin of maneuver for the negotiator. Randomness is an important element since environments change, and positions can reverse. Even when the negotiator has a clear and aligned focus, it's crucial to recognize when the rules of the game are redefined or when unforeseen risks increase the probability of a negative outcome. Both George Soros and Ron Johnson could have opposite reputations if randomness had provided opposite results to reality. Randomness is a constant factor in negotiations, and in this context, even with a determined focus, it's essential to monitor each step, ensuring that the path and criteria adopted are valid. Rationality and statistics assist negotiators in having numerical data and allow, in the face of changes, the focus and approach to be revised.

Emotional pressure can lead negotiators to make mistakes, so to minimize it, it's necessary to rely on rational foundations and possibilities, recognizing and monitoring randomness. The negotiator should always consider different scenarios, both positive and negative, and reassess them as the negotiation progresses. Unplanned concessions can arise during the process, new variables can come into play, and new external perceptions and expectations can create complexities. A negotiator needs to understand that advances don't necessarily mean only gains; losses are also part of the process as long as they contribute to achieving the established focus. In a business environment, negotiations don't occur in isolation, and failures can occur due to randomness and probability. However, negotiators need to take risks as long as these risks don't result in disastrous consequences for the business.

Negotiators can be involved in large mergers and acquisitions or be responsible for procurement categories or sales segments. Each business context has its relevance, but this doesn't determine how a negotiator should plan their negotiations and outcomes. Emotional pressure needs to be viewed with discernment, and a negotiator should be careful when addressing counterparts, avoiding basing their actions solely on authorities' expectations, provisions of overestimated results, and reactivity. Negotiation plays a fundamental role in all aspects, not just the final outcome. Therefore, understanding the negotiation format through game theory, understanding emotional manipulations, and relying on rational models that allow for building one's own perceptions are very powerful. Human cognitive processing should be supported by statistical foundations to ensure that randomness is not a surprise, and if it occurs, the negotiator should reassess the new possible scenarios while maintaining the focus.

Maintaining focus is a skill that involves the ability to say "no." In a negotiation, it's the ability to recognize what is relevant, allowing concessions on non-essential variables to promote progress. Deadlocks occur when relevant variables are disputed, and it's at that moment that creative solutions can create new possibilities. The goal is not necessarily to achieve a "win-win" but to advance in the negotiation toward the established focus. Emotional triggers, such as loss aversion and social acceptance, must be managed, ensuring that coherence is maintained and avoiding future dissimulations. An outcome with a defined focus involves considering various scenarios, all directed toward the stipulated objective. The decision between options takes into account economic and strategic criteria, using reverse logic to anticipate the best decision.

The cases presented in this book illustrate how negotiators approach counterparts, how outcomes are perceived by society, and what economic benefits and damages are brought to each side of the negotiation table. While emotional aspects are present in the mentioned cases, experienced negotiators are expected to base their decisions on rational assessments before making proposals, concessions, or closing deals. Emotion will always be a challenge for negotiators as it's an intrinsic part of human nature; however, it's essential to recognize emotional manipulation to avoid pitfalls. Emotion also plays a significant role in communication between parties, which is crucial to advancing in the negotiation. However, a negotiation should be grounded in rational aspects, and it's logic that ensures a coherent flow, anticipating criteria, assumptions, and possible outcomes. Statistics offer a more professional approach, anticipating trends and patterns and allowing the negotiator to adjust the negotiation in a broader context, associating probabilities, risks, and emotional measurements.

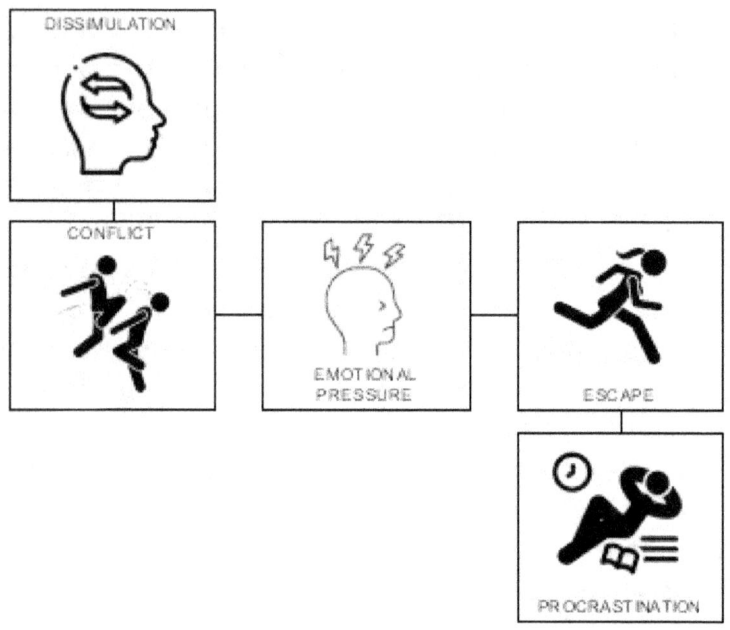

Focus remains the central element in a negotiation, and game theory allows for the development of possibilities and the recognition of opponents' strategies. By understanding counterparts' intentions through models of cooperation and conflict, what is said at the negotiation table is analyzed rationally, consolidating reactions and positions in a model where players reveal their strategies to deal with concessions, arguments, and offers. Negotiation is not a gift but a skill that must be developed. In it, emotional associations, effective communication, logical planning, understanding of rules, and consideration of scenarios ensure that a negotiator can adapt and advance with a focus on an outcome that, even in the face of randomness, will not result in irreparable consequences. The tools available for negotiation are infinite, and creative approaches will emerge, but emotional manipulation will always be part of human nature, even if disguised. A professional negotiator creates their own negotiation style, grounded in ethical principles and focused on achieving their goal, without necessarily seeking a "win-win." A good negotiator balances results, grounds their arguments in logic, and adapts to emotions and logical conditions of the moment.

About the Author

Mauricio Furtado is passionate about solving problems and saw the field of procurement as a perfect puzzle. His unique approach allows him to navigate business with creativity, addressing operational, tactical, and strategic aspects with consistent results. Mauricio has had the opportunity to participate in hundreds of negotiations, some of them extremely complex.

His negotiations have spanned the globe, enabling him to experience cultural approaches, business relationships, and the concept of win-win for various procurement and sales professionals. His experience is global, always working for billion-dollar multinational companies, some of them leaders in their industries, which has allowed him to understand expectations, approaches, and business failures around the world, both from colleagues and counterparts. Mauricio has witnessed turnarounds and unusual attempts to manipulate decisions.

About Hardcore

The concept was born from the compilation of numerous negotiations spanning over 20 years, where emotional approaches were always weakened by reason. Studying ways to adapt without letting emotion take over behavior ensured unexpected results and reactions. The standard approach of asking for discounts or increases, emphasizing partnership and "win-win," brought forth a reflection that deconstructs simplified approaches, mirroring techniques, empathy, and emotional control in favor of a technical approach, where logic, statistics, and game theory teach how to behave in challenging environments.

Hardcore aims to anticipate situations, knowing that when humans have access to possibilities, there is a greater chance of emotional control. The acquired knowledge and dedication to studying rarely used rational techniques have yielded consistent results, setting apart professionals who were interested in delving deep and applying them.

Carlos Mauricio Furtado

About the Book

The book offers an innovative perspective on negotiation, going beyond the traditional win-win approach and emotional techniques. It addresses serious experiments in irrationality, manipulation, and influence to show how susceptible we are to errors if we rely solely on emotion as a guide. The book has a rational focus and demonstrates, through various cases, that the use of logic, statistics, and game theory provides a significant advantage in any negotiation.

The book goes further by associating procrastination and a focus on prevailing conditions in relationships and business negotiations. In it, many examples of negotiations that have become public and business-related are used as a backdrop to present the fundamentals of rationality in real conditions, allowing the reader to associate and interpret their findings in real negotiations, considering that history repeats itself in different contexts and proportions.

www.ingramcontent.com/pod-product-compliance
Lightning Source LLC
Chambersburg PA
CBHW070115010626
45794CB00013B/1629